K   Ed
       72g

issued at the
Centennial of
the N. J. Ed. Assn.

The Story Of An Organization

Prepared by

LAURENCE B. JOHNSON

For the Centennial

of the

NEW JERSEY EDUCATION ASSOCIATION

180 W. State Street   Trenton, N. J.

100 Years Ago

In 1853 Uncle Tom's Cabin was just starting to become a best seller and My Old Kentucky Home was newly published. The Washington monument was under construction, as were the north and south wings of the nation's capitol. Admiral Perry landed in Japan, and New York was entranced by the Crystal Palace exhibition. Franklin Pierce was President.

New Jersey's population was less than half a million, of whom some 200 were still slaves. There were no Republicans in the State; non-Democrats were the "Opposition" or "Anti-Nebraska" party. The $30,000 annual payment to the State by the Joint Companies (Delaware and Raritan Canal and the Penna. Railroad) covered most of the State's budget. The Morris Canal from Phillipsburg to Jersey City was at the height of its operation with its 23 inclined planes and 28 regular locks. Plank roads were hailed as the ultimate answer for other forms of transportation.

The State had barely 100,000 school children and some 1500 teachers, of whom two out of three were men. The schools of the day come to life a century later in the reports of the State Superintendents. That office was created in 1846 as part of a basic school law which, with minor amendments, served the State for two decades. The early superintendents, T. F. King and John H. Phillips, were medical men, to whose concern for education New Jersey owes much. In addition to their own forthright comments on school conditions, their reports contain statements from local superintendents. These were not professional educators, but the citizens primarily responsible in the various townships for the administration and enforcement of the school laws.

THE SCHOOL HOUSES

The school buildings of a century ago offered a wider range of contrast than those of today. New Brunswick had just completed "a very beautiful and commodious school edifice, . . . which for convenience and symetry, is believed to be far superior to any other school in the state." In this building, at the end of that same year, the State Teachers Association was to be organized.

Newark had some 16 public schools, seven for boys, seven for girls, one primary and one colored. The Legislature had just passed an act to incorporate its Board of Education, and the city had paid $5,000 for a 90x125 foot lot on which its new high school building was "under cover." Jersey City remodeled a building "to very great advantage" with "sliding doors for the purpose of dividing up the schoolrooms at pleasure into recitation rooms."

Elizabeth had central heating problems. "The first and second stories are warmed by steam. This apparatus saved the city fuel, but from the beginning has been a source of great annoyance. The heating surface, until recently (1861) was sheet-iron radiators, which, from their tendency to rust, were constantly out of repair. These have been taken away, and substantial coils of iron pipe substituted. But owing to a defect in their construction, they are attended by a disagreeable noise."

Bᴜᴛ ᴛʜᴇsᴇ were the exceptions. State Superintendent King says, in 1848.

"A merciful man, being merciful to his beast, would not winter his horse in places appropriated at present for district school houses. Let him travel over our state, in what direction he will, and if he sees a building, some sixteen feet by twenty, with the clap boards off in some places, in others hanging by a single nail, fluttering to every breeze. the roof open. the door with one hinge, and that a leather one, the windows wanting glass.

but abounding in old hats, caps and cloaks, or copy books, he may with tolerable certainty set it down for a country school house—if it is located at the junction of two or more roads, in a low wet spot, with no fence around it, and no appurtenances attached—he may be certain of it, and enter freely . . . he will find the benches without backs, too narrow for comfort, and too high for the majority of the little ones, whose feet hang dangling, without support, . . . the desks are of all sizes and all varieties, the tops carved by the ingenuity of some aspiring architect, into all manner of forms and figures."

A committee, appointed by the Sussex County Educational Society, states "with perfect confidence, that there is not a school house in the county fit for the purposes to which it is appropriated." In Atlantic County "without adornment and without paint, they stand forth the sorrowful and weather-beaten monuments of ignorance, parsimony, and public neglect."

Thomas C. Rogers, superintendent in Waterford of Camden County, is more impassioned:

"Who can deny the fact, that the state penitentiary does now, present more inducements for a horse thief to seek his subsistence and comfort in its rooms, than any common school or academy, founded and supported by the state, offers to an aspiring youth, athirst for knowledge, to resort thither for the enlightment and nourishment of his immortal mind."

A year later he says, "if the trustees of the several districts would give only the degree of attention to them that farmers must to a house for their pigs, we should have warmer houses in some places, and cleaner ones in others."

In Middlesex County "there are school houses that the farmers would not use for stables; and yet, with all their wealth, they are willing to send their children there to obtain an education, exposed to the dampness of the storm and the severity of the cold."

Some districts had none at all. In Bordentown "the places appropriated to school purposes are either apartments in buildings erected for private residences, or built by private enterprise, with scarcely any regard to ventilation, light, etc., so necessary for the health and progress of a pupil. The consequence is, that should the trustees (as has been the case) desire to revoke a teacher's license and employ another teacher, they are restrained from so doing by the fact that the unworthy teacher has exclusive possession of the only available school building not occupied, and the trustees find themselves unable to procure a suitable room for the new one."

And in a Belleville district "containing more than 500 children of legal school age," the school trustees report that

"without their consent, and against their remonstrance, the public school house, after said trustees had refused to entertain an application for the purchase of it, was torn down on the night of July 11th of the present year."

THE TEACHERS

Teaching in 1853, was just beginning to emerge as a profession. Licensing had only recently been introduced; local superintendents were charged with the issuance of certificates, and trustees were not supposed to hire or pay salaries to those who did not obtain such licenses. The town superintendents complain much, however, both of the hiring of unlicensed teachers and of the poor quality of those seeking their approval. State Superintendent Phillips states the general case.

"One of the greatest difficulties experienced by the school officers, is to procure good and competent teachers; and whilst we have many in the state who fill the important office with honor to themselves and usefulness to the community, there are others, and unfortunately the larger number, who are incompetent for the performance of the duties they are expected to execute. In a great majority of cases, even those who possess the necessary amount of information are ignorant of the best methods of imparting it to others; they having had no experience in conducting a school, are consequently ignorant of the many thousand avenues to the youthful mind, and consequently labor without method and without success."

A local superintendent notes that "the time has scarcely yet past when teaching was supposed to be a calling which anyone could at any time take up. The man who failed in business, and knew nothing else to which he could so readily turn his hands, imagined himself fully qualified to 'teach the young idea how to shoot' if he could only read a little, write any sort of a hand, cypher as far as the 'rule of three,' and spell correctly book in hand, so as to be sure not to miss when hearing the class . . . deficiency in learning, in correct enunciation and emphasis, was fully compensated, in the estimation of most, by his dexterous use of the ferrule or birch."

"With the increasing interest in education, there is also an increase of difficulties," says the head of the Chatham schools. "The general character of the teachers is good, and their morality I have endeavored to be cautious about ascertaining," says another superintendent. Others were not so fearful:

"I have licensed only about one quarter of those who have applied; objections, either in qualifications as teachers, or in character as regards morals, having been too numerous to pass over."

And Mr. Rogers, whose comments on school buildings were so vitriolic, gives a vivid picture of a local examination:

"Of four, which are all who have applied to me for license, not one has been considered competent to teach even a primary school; although circumstances have compelled me to give a qualified license for three months, to two of them. The last one that applied, a young man of respectable appearance, who had taught school two quarters, (a relative of the trustee who brought him), could not pass in reading, or spelling, or arithmetic as far as compound numbers—more was not attempted. In reading; words mispronounced—in spelling; such words as 'settlers,' 'intelligence,' 'preferred,' taken from a lesson just read were missed, some at the third trial—in defining; '*min*ute', 'min*ute*', 'princi*pal*' and 'princi*ple*', which also occurred in the reading exercise, were not explained—and to top the whole, the trustees pronounced the asking of such questions, with others on the principles of arithmetic, and on his method of conducting recitations, 'all a fol-de-rol,' and 'something new in the world;' and the superintendent denounced as being 'too severe,' and as 'trying to prevent them from having a school.'"

Nevertheless the Hampton board passed a resolution stating "that teaching ought to be a profession, and that in employing teachers we will always give the preference to one who follows teaching as a business."

Dr. Phillips says firmly: "Teaching should be properly a distinct profession, for which the professor should be prepared by a due course of previous training . . . And the most efficient means in its accomplishment, will be the establishment, under proper regulations, of schools for the preparation and training of teachers."

There was a growing understanding of the relationship of teaching quality to salary. "There is but little attention paid to the qualifications of the teachers, provided he is a clever fellow, and will work cheap."

"The chief defect here is a lack of culture. Teachers are not far enough in advance of pupils to give that enthusiasm and thoroughness which otherwise might be imparted. This defect makes teaching laborious, and learning drudgery. The remedy for these evils I leave for wiser heads to propose. Parents do not pay for much, nor do they expect much."

"One thing I well know, that the standard of teaching is not as high generally as it ought to be.

**Brainerd School, in Mount Holly, is more than the
oldest school building in New Jersey. It was the first
building in which public education as we know it was
offered, starting in 1765. The New Jersey Society,
Colonial Dames of America, are now engaged in a
major restoration project on this building.**

although there is many honorable exceptions among
teachers; but I well know that if teachers could get
compensated for teaching that there would be more
good teachers."

THE ACTUAL SALARIES of teachers varied widely. Isaiah
Peckham, principal of Newark's high school, was
probably the highest paid professional educator in New
Jersey with $1027.28. Lodi, with a new building boasts
that "the salary paid the teacher (six hundred dollars
per annum) is considered sufficient to secure the services
of men of talent." The Superintendent justifies the salary
by noting:

"The inadequate compensation generally awarded
to our teachers is one of the greatest obstacles to
the prosperity of our schools. We must make the
profession attractive—make it sufficiently remun-
erative to induce the right class of men to engage in

it—men of proper tact and education, otherwise
we must continue to suffer the inevitable conse-
quences resulting from the labors of inexperienced
and second rate teachers—the cullings of New England and New York."

Wages of $600 and $1,000 were by no means standard,
however. In Hanover (Morris County),

"the average wages of teachers in this township,
for the past year, has been less than sixty dollars
per quarter. But one school pays fair mechanics'
wages to its teachers. In the majority of cases, the
male teachers, after paying for their board and
washing, will have left, as their compensation, only
about the same sum that our farmers pay for the
service of the better class of emigrant laborers on
their farms. Those who handle the pick and the
shovel on the public works receive better wages than
the majority of those who teach our children. So
long as this continues to be the case, it is vain to
expect much improvement in the character of our
public schools. Since there are so many other oc-
cupations requiring no greater amount of attention
and acquirements, which are so much more remun-
erative than teaching, our public schools must, of
necessity, to a considerable extent, be under the
tuition of incompetent or inefficient men . . . In
the present state of things, for a man to deliberately
propose to pursue the vocation of a teacher of public schools for life, would be almost sufficient to
prove that he was a man of disinterested benevo-
lence, or that he was unfit for the high and responsible vocation of teaching."

In many cases the money was not paid directly to the
teacher, but had to be collected by the teacher individually from parents. That practice is reflected in a Newton
comment:

"teachers are sure to find out those townships
which have school money to the extent of the law,
and as a matter of course prefer teaching in them
. . . Fifty dollars per quarter, in a rural district,
where the money can be drawn at once from the

town, is often better than seventy dollars to be collected from the employers."

Fifty years later Charles J. Baxter at the State Association's fiftieth anniversary remembered

"calling on a worthy citizen, who had sent a scapegrace of a boy to school now and then, and trying to collect $1.30. He said: 'That's an outrageous bill, our schools are costing too much money.' I had not the courage to dissent, because my heart told me that particular boy had not been benefited to the extent of $1.30. The next bill was $26.10. This was so much I had not the courage to ask for it. This particular patron called on me, (it is a joy to think of him yet) settled his bill and said he would have paid it most cheerfully had it been twice as much. He brought his children to school regularly. The third patron took my bill, pulled out the stand drawer and very critically compared his record of days' attendance with mine. He said: 'Well, your account is all right. I had the money ready for you yesterday.' I called on others who did not have the money 'ready for me yesterday.' Why, my friends, I have tuition fees coming up in the hills of Sussex yet."

At least one teacher included textbooks in his total wage.

"For the last five years I have been engaged in teaching . . . Two years ago I proposed to the trustees to teach for so much per scholar and find all the books, except copies. Convinced of the merits of McGuffey's books, I put them in place of the old and various kinds the children had been using. It produced a change highly satisfactory to all parties. I mention this, that those who design teaching for life, and are complaining of ill-adapted books, and cannot influence trustees and parents to furnish better, that they may know the only remedy I could find, that is, furnish themselves, as mechanics do, with their own tools, and charge accordingly."

Down in Greenwich Township, Cumberland County, stands a small stone schoolhouse that is now a home and headquarters for New Jersey artists. It has been well maintained, and is one of the most charming and picturesque of the old schools which were standing long before NJEA was founded.

The salaries of women teachers were of course lower than those of men. Many school districts made ends meet by hiring male teachers for the winter sessions, and women in the summer when the big boys would presumably be hard at work. Salem County sent this comment on the relationship of men and women teachers:

"The character of our schools we believe to be gradually improving, especially those taught by females . . . This state of things has been produced by the small compensation offered to teachers . . . Most of the females employed as teachers are such as have acquired an education to fit them for that business, and who intend following it; our male teachers are the sons of farmers and engage in teaching to fill up the time."

Not only the season shift, however, but the whole tradition of the times was in favor of frequent changes of teachers and positions. With eleven teachers, Upper

Freehold had only two that were employed for a second year. Hackensack reports that,

"Of nine districts, seven have changed teachers since April last, and some of them more than once. One of the remaining two districts has employed a teacher three and a half years, and the other two and three-quarter years. Frequent changes of teachers is, indisputably, a bad practice. Wherever these changes are most frequent, there is the least progress. The advantage resulting from the long retention of a good teacher, is at once apparent in the popularity and prosperity of the school. The practice, however, should not always be taken as evidence against the trustees. It, in many instances, only proves that good teachers are scarce, and that trustees are only making trials, in order to secure the services of a good one at last."

Another Bergen County superintendent says:

"Nothing can injure a school more than to suffer those interruptions which are necessarily made by frequent change of teachers. Although the school be not left vacant for a single week, yet from the fact that every teacher has his peculiarities, both in his method of teaching and in his natural disposition, it distracts the minds and affections of children too much, if at every quarter or half year they are compelled to study the character of a strange person, and to arrive at the important conclusion, whether they can love (not merely like) him or not."

WHAT WAS TAUGHT

The Superintendent in Upper Freehold had a statistical mind. From him, in 1853, we get the following breakdown of what his 528 pupils were studying:

"332 is the average number in daily attendance 36 learn the alphabet; 66 learn to spell without being able to read; 117 learn to read; 306 learn to write; 112 learn arithmetic, but not beyond simple division; 182 learn arithmetic beyond simple division; 214 learn geography; 94 learn English grammar; 190 learn to define words; 21 learn algebra; 24 learn history; 5 learn geometry; 25 learn natural philosophy; 3 learn surveying; 10 learn mensuration."

In Hohokus: "The branches of education taught in our schools are reading, writing, arithmetic and geography. It is to be regretted that, either owing to the unyielding prejudice of parents or the lamentable neglect on the part of teachers, grammar does not constitute a more prominent feature in the course of study adopted in the schools, as well as the pleasing and profitable study of some of the natural sciences—such as natural philosophy, chemistry, physiology, etc., which by a simple mode of instruction, with the assistance of the lucid explanations of suitable text-books, might be made comprehensible to quite young scholars. The introduction of mental arithmetic has become universal to our schools . . . Penmanship, although a universal branch of study, is not generally practised or taught according to system, but on the principle of imitation, or the mere option of the scholar."

Then, as now, penmanship was a subject of dispute and controversy:

"You scarcely find a teacher capable of writing a good, fair copy hand, and instructing a class in the principles of the art . . . This degeneracy in the art of writing has had a bad effect on spelling. You cannot at this day, from much of the writing you see, even among teachers, judge whether it is spelled right or wrong, and are consequently cut short of another means of judging a man's acquirements, as it would be rather out of fashion to write a legible hand."

The curriculum was expanding however. In Mercer County

"The studies of natural philosophy, algebra, geometry, and vocal music have been introduced with success during the past year, and it is believed with great advantage to the school. The scholars manifest a warm interest in these branches, and, though the last possesses not the practical utility of the others, it is hoped that it will contribute to refine the feelings—the culture of which should not, as it too frequently is, be lightly regarded."

Advocates of history complain that the pupils "appear about as much enlightened in regard to the past as to the future." Others sought greater emphasis upon the Bible.

"Visible illustrations are much more relied upon by teachers now than formerly, and by means of the black-board, with which nearly every district is provided, either the property of the district or the teacher, a class of fifteen or twenty may be and are as easily instructed, and on account of the saving of time, very much more thoroughly instructed than one scholar could be under the old process."

In some districts colored children were a problem. Perth Amboy was boldly planning to "integrate" them, on the ground that "part of the public money of right belongs to them, and they should not in justice be deprived of it." In another district, however, a committee was appointed "to see if they cannot be removed."

The question of parochial schools was also present. In Belleville,

"Our Catholic neighbors wish to be provided for by themselves. They have petitioned me to apportion to them part of the school moneys in my hands, for the support of their schools. I have found no authority so to do. They again petition me to district them in such a way that they manage their own concerns."

Children were being sent to school at early ages. A Bergen County superintendent observes, however, that "a child entered in school at the age of eight years, will be as far advanced at thirteen, as one of equal capacity entered at the age of five years . . . I do not suppose our rulers wish to convert our teachers into childs-nurses or our school rooms into nurseries." Another says,

"I think that six or seven is young enough for a child to commence school, particularly if the bench is without a back."

In this school, in Bordentown, Clara Barton taught before she became the driving force behind the American Red Cross. It is maintained by the Bordentown Manual Training School for the State Department of Education.

METHODS AND DISCIPLINE

Discipline is "moral suasion, rewards, and the rod combined" reports one realistic superintendent. The schools of 1853 ranged from the most primitive methods of instruction and discipline to those which smack of the best modern thinking.

Down in Monmouth County, near Freehold, the idealistic, socialized North American Phalanx was contributing much beside the "bloomer girl" to our civilization. In its views of a "normal education" a leading idea was:

"That the senses are first active, that children are curious to know the qualities of things by sight and touch, are desirous to do the things that they see their elders perform; consequently that the development of the body and its powers is first to be cared for, consequently that as an educational basis, we must organize the various industries of life, and to

which each child must have free access, so that
each may find such vocations as he is best fitted to
perform."

Our friend Mr. Rogers says:

"Whether it is right or not, we know that children
have a good deal to say, and not unjustly too, about
this matter of going to school. We know that when
they are interested in the school and schoolroom
exercises, they love to go there; and that when these
things are unpleasant, they will not go, or rather,
in most cases, do not."

The normal picture may well have been that given in
Upper Freehold, where

"Our teachers class the scholars as far as practic-
able, have them to recite in concert, exercise on the
blackboard, sing geography and their tables, and
after much oral instruction are questioned and examined as to their understanding of the branches
they study. This however must be received with
some exceptions. Quietness and order are apparent
in some schools; noise and inattention in others.
The rod is used to a moderate extent in some, in
others not at all."

There was a growing objection to corporal punishment. From Cape May comes this description of a
teacher:

"Our school has been taught about ten months in
a year since the spring of 1851, by a gentleman
who is unquestionably a scholar of a high order,
and a good teacher; yet, of course, not without
his faults; among which, in my humble opinion,
may be named too great severity, and too frequent
use of the rod. I am not one of those who object
to its use altogether, but . . . I am fully convinced
that but little corporal punishment, with other good
management, will insure better order, either in
school or the family."

ORGANIZATION

Each township had an elected superintendent, from
whose reports come many of these pictures of school
conditions. These had the authority to license teachers,

to divide the township into school districts, and to call district meetings for the election of School Trustees. The latter hired the teachers, provided for school houses, and listed the children to be educated.

Superintendents were often critical of the Trustees.

"It would have been gratifying to have recognized more zeal and interest manifested by trustees in some of the districts. Much responsibility is attached to these officers . . . The unaided, singlehanded services of the superintendent will avail but little. The united, zealous and constant efforts of a board of trustees, being more nearly and personally interested, would accomplish much."

From Raritan: "There is one obstacle in the way of the proper improvement of public schools, which obstacle it will take at least one generation to fully remove. It is the ignorance of school officers. In some districts there are none who are properly qualified to be school trustees. They have never seen a well conducted school. Time alone can remedy this difficulty. The children of such trustees as we have, will, it is to be hoped, make in due time better trustees than their fathers are."

From North Brunswick: "Thank heaven! there is some prospect for our schools in this township, even though a *generation* (apparently) must be educated before we can have a set of decent school trustees."

And from Wall Township this reverberation of an early political controversy:

"Two cases occurred last spring in this town where the trustees were divided as to the teachers. Efforts were made to elect trustees to expel the teachers employed by former trustees and regularly licensed. The school house was closed and locked; one of the teachers prosecuted the trustees for the full term. Judgment in favor of the teacher by a jury . . . I am still of the opinion that females would make the best trustees. I know of no law to prevent it."

FINANCING THE SCHOOLS

The idea of free public school education was growing but its full realization was nearly a quarter-century away. The State appropriated $80,000 a year for schools. It was apportioned among the counties:

> "In the ratio of the population thereof as ascertained by the last preceding census, and authorizing the people to supply by taxes voluntarily imposed, such further sum of money as they may deem proper for the support of public schools, not exceeding three dollars for each child contained in the lists transmitted by the several district trustees to the Town Superintendents."

The law authorized the establishment of free schools when "two-thirds of the taxable inhabitants . . . shall so determine." More common, however, were the "rate-bills" by which parents contributed toward the education of their own children. In many districts, as we have seen, the teachers were required to collect their own accounts.

From Orange comes this account of school finances:

> "None of our schools are absolutely free; a fee is received from the scholars varying from forty-five cents to one dollar, according to the exigencies of each district . . . In our largest district each pupil brings his ticket which he has procured of the trustees at 45 cents, and this entitles him to his place in the school for a quarter. In this district the books and contingent expenses are furnished by the trustees, and are computed to be about equivalent to the assessment of forty-five cents, so that the tuition may be considered virtually free. . . . But while the system of free schools is decidedly gaining in popular favor, there is, and is likely to be, a yearly struggle between the taxpayers and the supposed beneficiaries of the law."

The idea of free education was not universally endorsed, even by those closest to the schools. The New Harrington superintendent wrote in 1851:

Oak Summit School, in Hunterdon County, was built in 1852, closed in 1949, and reopened in September 1952 to meet the emergency caused by increasing school enrollments in Kingwood Township.

"It is to be hoped that this will be the last year of free schools in this town, as it has been the first."

State Superintendent Phillips defended local support in these words:

"There are many warm friends of education, who are of the opinion that some equivalent should be demanded from the people, to entitle them to the bounty of the state, believing that if the entire expense of conducting the schools is met by the state, the citizens will look upon them with indifference, and finally lose all interest in their management. They are of opinion that schools flourish best in those townships where a large proportion of the expense is defrayed by a voluntary assessment; and that, in order not only to increase the amount, but the interest in the successful operation of the schools, whatever the state gives should be met by a certain fixed proportion to be raised by the townships. Notwithstanding this difference, all agree that a much larger appropriation should be made by the state."

The raising of local taxes for schools involved problems. In one school district:

"The town meeting voted to raise one thousand and fifty dollars; about two dollars per scholar. But as this sum was more than our heavy tax payers were willing to have assessed upon their property, it was voted almost unanimously to compromise the matter by assessing about one half of this amount upon persons, at the rate of fifty cents upon married men, and one dollar and fifty cents upon single men. This measure gave very general satisfaction, until the legality of it was questioned and agitated, and since then, numbers of our young men refuse to submit to the order of the town meeting."

There were strong advocates of state school aid, however. In Camden:

"A poll tax of one dollar is assessed upon every male inhabitant of the city, for school purposes . . . I believe it to be the desire of 'friends of education of the masses' in this section, that a law should be enacted, by which schools should be supported directly by the state revenues, and that property should contribute to the maintenance of that government which guarantees its peaceable possession."

Another superintendent writes: "Another great defect, is the manner of taxation for the support of schools; some of the money being raised by the state, some by the township, and the remainder by those who patronize the schools. It should, in my opinion, be so arranged as to have the money all raised by a state tax, that tax to be raised upon the whole property of the state."

And a third says: "The inhabitants generally are favorable to popular education, but objections exist in the minds of many as to the mode by which the means for the maintenance of free schools is raised. What they desire is that the state shall appropriate an amount sufficient to give every child the benefits of a common school education, and for whatever deficiency there may be in the state treasury for the support of the government, they are willing to be taxed."

T HE IDEA of equalization of educational opportunity
was wide-spread. Here are two statements of the case,
which have a curiously modern ring:

"A very respectable portion of the people in this
township believe that the state school fund should
be enlarged. Indeed, this appears to be the correct
method, and the only one that can be of great public
utility. For instance, some of the townships in this
state are far more opulent than others; according
to the provisions of the present law, the rich townships can easily raise the amount allowed thereby,
while the burden of raising the same amount per
scholar would be entirely too heavy upon the poorer
townships. The consequence must be that the poor
children of poor townships will grow up without
an education; and those children, too, some of whom
might be qualified to fill the highest stations in
society, Whereas, if the state fund was augmented,
and the money distributed according to the annual
enumeration of the children of legal age capable of
attending school, it would more equally throw the
means of education within the reach of all; and
why not educate all the children of the state? . . .
In a government like ours, the perpetuity of our
institutions depends upon the intelligence of the
citizens, and it is for the future benefit of each
individual child, that the greatest possible number
of his or her contemporaries be well informed and
properly trained up.

"As it now stands, our schools, if free, must be
made so by township and district assessment, the
state fund being a trifle, (its great value being its
certainty). One township may raise a large sum by
tax, and the adjoining townships none . . . one
district may keep the school open free while their
next neighboring school is closed for want of willingness to be taxed. It may be said, if they have
not the benefits, they do not bear the burden; but
it is made a state institution, for the benefit of the
children of the state, the people of the state to
support it; the benefit ought to be then extended to

all children, and the duty of supporting this state institution imposed upon all the people. There is no equality of taxation in the small districted assessments. One district may have thrice as many children as its neighboring district of equal or greater wealth, and I believe, it is true, generally, that divisions numbering the most children, have the least wealth to educate them. 'Flocks and herds' of this kind are peculiarly the property of the poor, and are very unproductive of anything to support a teacher, though they may form a very good school. In every county may be found instances of poor and populous districts. . . . The remedy is to make schools free throughout the state by state appropriation, raise the money by general tax, or appropriate the income of the state for the purpose, and support the government by direct taxation. The hundreds who complain of the school tax never did and never will object to paying state tax; this would prevent discordant jarrings between rich and poor, simplify the law, make taxation more equitable, because more general, and render the support of free schools in the state certain, permanent, and universal."

The broad case for free public schools was that made by State Superintendent King in 1848:

"Let not those who have completed the education of their children, nor those who have none, startle at the proposition to tax their property for the benefit of their neighbor's offspring; let them not suppose that it is unjust or oppressive, as it is neither. Fellow citizens are all equally interested in the general diffusion of knowledge, as tending to secure the permanency of our peculiar institutions, for it has been truly remarked, that 'a well educated people can never be other than free.' "

CITIZEN INTEREST

"If a farmer hires a hand to till his soil or feed his swine, he will occasionally stroll into his field, or walk to his styes; but does he ever enter the school house in which his children are being educated; or does he ever catechise them concerning their studies?"

So writes a New Hanover superintendent. In Hamilton Township:

"The question, 'Do parents visit your school?' has been asked of every teacher. It has been deemed a matter of much importance by those who have had the most experience in teaching, that parents would do much by occasionally visiting the schools; it would encourage and strengthen the teacher in his position, by a community of feeling between him and his employers; their presence would stimulate their children to application and perseverance. I regret to state that a negative answer has almost invariably been given."

"Formerly it was a rare thing for any person to visit the school, and frequently whole terms would pass away without an individual entering the school-room, save the superintendent. Now it is common for parents to call upon the teacher and see how the school is progressing."

Actually, however, there was a deep, wide-spread citizen interest in public education. This was the motive power in virtually every step forward, including the founding of the State Teachers Association itself.

As early as 1828 a "convention" in Trenton appointed a Central Committee on Education to canvass the State and collect statistics from every county. Similar committees grew up in many townships and counties to aid the Central Committee. The reports, however, showed that over one-third of the children in the state were without schooling.

A decade later, and despite legislation growing out of the earlier activity, citizen interest was still strong. Another State Convention of the Friends of Education met in Trenton on January 16, 1838. It declared that the school laws were defective and ought to be repealed. It recommended the appointment of a State Superintendent of Common Schools, and the abolition of pauper schools. It appointed a committee, with Rev. George W.

Newark High School at Washington and Linden Streets, had Isaiah Peckham, an NJEA founder, as its principal. Boys were taught on the second floor, girls on the third. Normal classes were held here on Saturdays.

Doane, Bishop of New Jersey, as chairman, to issue an address to the people. This address was reprinted by the New Jersey Education Association in 1938 on the anniversary of its issuance. In it Bishop Doane said:

"Tax yourselves for the support of common schools, and you will never be in danger of taxation from a foreign power. You will need less taxation for the support of pauperism and the punishment of crime. Look to your schoolhouses. See that they are convenient of access, that they are comfortable, that they are neat and tasteful. Look to the teachers. See that they are taught themselves and apt to teach—men that fear God and love their country. See that they are well accommodated, well treated, well remunerated. Respect them and they will respect themselves, and your children will respect them. Look well to the scholars. Remember you are to grow old among them. Remember you are to die and leave your country in their hands."

Out of this movement grew, in the 1840's, major

revisions of the State school law, creation of the State Superintendency, and the writing of the State School Fund into the Constitution of 1844.

This citizen interest was reflected in the newspapers of the day. In 1848 Superintendent T. F. King said in his annual report:

"The editors of our public papers have in all cases lent the aid of their columns to those who wished to address the public mind upon the subject of general education. They have given a free insertion to all notices calling public meetings; and more important still, have generally lent their own aid in support of popular education. When it is considered how important the influence is, which is exercised by the public press of our country upon any popular movement . . . it must be acknowledged that no influence can be brought to bear, which will act with more force upon the public mind than that of the press. How fortunate then, for us, that the press of our state has lent its aid in favor of popular education; that it has sent forth its daily or weekly messengers with words of inspiring hope, calling upon the better principles of our nature to awaken."

By 1853, however, the time was ripe for another revival of citizen activity. From his office-home in Pennington State Superintendent John H. Phillips sent out the following notice:

"A convention of the friends of education will be held in the city of Trenton on Thursday, the 20th day of October next, at 10 o'clock a.m. The object of the convention is the promotion of the cause of common school education. The friends of the cause throughout the state are invited to attend."

Of that meeting held in Temperance Hall, he reports:

"Although it was convened under somewhat unfavorable circumstances, at a season when, from political and other considerations, the attendance was not as large as the importance of the occasion demanded, yet its proceedings were of a highly interesting and important character; evincing not only the strong interest felt in this important subject, but the consideration of the means of improving and perfecting our common school system, as well as the extension and diffusion of useful knowledge among the people."

That meeting adopted resolutions urging:

1. Free education everywhere.
2. Organization of associations of teachers and and friends of education in every county and every town.
3. A full-time State Superintendent of Schools at a salary of $1,500 annually.
4. State appropriation of $100 for each county holding an annual institute.
5. Appropriation to each district for a school library.
6. Adoption of a State educational journal.

The State Educational Journal favored by the Convention was the *New Jersey Life Boat and Literary Standard*, later known as the *New Jersey Literary Standard*; its editors were Isaiah Peckham and William R. Howell, Newark teachers.

The organization of the State Teachers Association was clearly an outgrowth of this meeting and its second resolution. Two months later the teachers themselves were called together in New Brunswick.

The Early Years

T EACHER associations were not new in 1853. As early
as 1848 Dr. King, State Superintendent, writes in his
annual report:

> "In most of the counties of the state, 'County
> Associations' have been formed, for the promotion
> of public school education, composed of the teachers
> and friends of education, in the respective counties.
> At these associations, whose meetings are generally
> quarterly, subjects of interest to the teacher and the
> parent are introduced, and methods of instructing
> and imparting information communicated, and other
> matters of importance to all discussed. At some of
> these quarterly meetings, (as is the case in Essex
> County,) the teachers of the township in which the
> meeting is held, bring forward classes of children
> from their schools, the better to illustrate their own
> method of teaching, and also draw out information
> from others present. This plan has been found to
> increase the interest taken in these meetings, and to
> advance the children attending the various schools,
> and is confidently recommended to the favorable
> notice of those associations which have not adopted
> it. At many of these meetings the most intelligent
> and influential of the inhabitants have been present
> and, as honorary members, taken part in the exer-
> cises, and they are daily growing in favor, and the
> most elevated are willing to lend a helping hand.
> The present Governor of our state is an active mem-
> ber and president of the Sussex County association."

Local as well as county groups were informed. Mr.
Rogers reports in 1853 that

> "Our teachers met at the house of the superinten-
> dent to consider what they could do for each other
> and for the schools in the township. One resolution

of that meeting was, to form a township association of teachers, which has since been done. The association has met three times, holding its meetings on the first Saturday of each month.

"They have formed a constitution & c.: and extend to the superintendents and teachers in other townships, the invitation to come and improve with them. None but teachers, or those who have been, can become members of the association; and one article of the constitution requires all the members to form themselves into a class or classes of scholars, who shall recite at each monthly meeting of the association on some branch of common school instruction, which the class at a previous meeting shall have agreed upon; and the teacher for the occasion shall be some member of the class to be chosen on the day of recitation. This rule has, for three meetings, worked admirably. Our recitations, thus far, have been upon the alphabet, oral spelling, and analysing words. How long before we shall take up something else I cannot say; but one thing is quite certain, not one of us will leave this regretting that it was taken up, or that so much time has been bestowed upon it."

THE FOUNDING

The notice calling the first state-wide meeting of New Jersey teachers was signed by C. C. Hoagland, John B. Thompson, and John T. Clark. It says:

"The undersigned, in behalf of many Teachers present at the late Educational Convention at Trenton, respectfully invite the Teachers of New Jersey to meet in the city of New Brunswick on WEDNESDAY, the 28th of December next, at 11 o'clock A. M. for the purpose of forming a State Teachers' Association, and for the consideration of business incident thereto."

Of the meeting the State Gazette reports:

"TEACHERS' CONVENTION—This convention assembled yesterday at New Brunswick. Eight*

---

*Apparently Essex, Sussex, Morris, Hunterdon, Somerset, Middlesex, Mercer and Burlington.

counties were represented, and about fifty teachers were present.

"After effecting a temporary organization at 11 o'clock on Wednesday by the appointment of Nathan Hedges as Chairman and the appointment of a business committee, the convention adjourned until after dinner.

"In the afternoon the business Committee reported a Constitution which was taken up and acted upon article by article. The discussion on its main features occupied most of the session. The following is a synopsis: Members—only those actively engaged in teaching; school officers being eligible to honorary membership. Officers, to consist of a President, two Vice Presidents, three Secretaries and a Treasurer. Annual meeting in the last week of December. County Associations may become auxiliary.

"In the evening the Association met and proceeded to its first election of officers, which resulted in the following choice:

President—R. L. Cooke, of Essex.

Vice-Presidents—J. T. Clarke of Middlesex and Isaiah Peckham of Newark.

Cor'g. Sec'y.—David Cole of Mercer.

Rec. Sec'y.—J. H. Burnham, of Burlington and U. N. Cox of Morris.

Treasurer—O. A. Kibbe, of Somerset.

"The election was followed by the reading of an excellent Essay by Mr. David Cole. The following resolution was presented, discussed and adopted:

Resolved, That the office of State Superintendent of the Public Schools in this State should be filled only by a practical teacher."

In his annual report for 1853 Dr. Phillips says:

"A convention of the teachers of the state was held in the city of New Brunswick, under highly favorable and auspicious circumstances; *and availing themselves of the principle of associated action in the accomplishment of the great and good work in which they are engaged,* they became permanently organized as an association, prepared to enter with renewed vigor upon a future, yet I trust brighter and more glorious career of prosperity and usefulness."

A MORE INFORMAL picture of that first meeting and the early leaders appears in the reminiscences of John Bodine Thompson at the 50th anniversary meeting of the New Jersey State Teachers Association. He said:

"It was a very enthusiastic meeting. Every one had his ideal and his opinion of the best method to realize it. And every one was quite aware that his ideal could be realized only by the hearty cooperation of all. Nathan Hedges, the oldest teacher present, was chosen to preside. The preamble (of the constitution) accurately stated the motives of the founders: 'The teachers of the State of New Jersey, regarding themselves as responsible agents for conducting the educational system, and persuaded that union of feeling and concert would greatly assist them in bearing the responsibility, do hereby agree to form themselves into an association to be governed by the following constitution.' From that day to this no convention of the friends of education in New Jersey has been necessary.

"Robert Latimer Cooke was the son of Mrs. Harriet B. Cooke, from whose famous school in Bloomfield two thousand educated women went forth to bless the communities in which their lots were cast. After graduating from college he studied law, but soon abandoned his profession to become a teacher, first at Princeton, and finally in the school over which his mother so long presided. A man of unusual culture and refinement. he went from place to place pleading for better educational advantages for children and youth. I heard him first at the teachers' institute in Somerville in 1849, where he set before us better ideals that we had known before, and showed us the way to realize them. I thought then, as I think now, that I had never seen a better example of the suaviter in modo along with the *fortiter in re*. Later, his esthetic tastes found gratifi-

cation in his connection with the department of
public parks in the city of New York. He was
drowned by a tidal wave off Fire Island, August 11,
1877.

"The first vice-presidents of the association were
John T. Clark, of New Brunswick, and Isaiah Peckham, of Newark. Mr. Clark was the popular principal of the school where the meeting was held, and
was afterward seriously talked of for the principalship of the State Normal School. Failing to secure
this, he removed to one of the Western States, where
he became useful and influential in a judicial capacity.

"The other vice-president, Isaiah Peckham, was
just thirty years of age, and had already been pro-
moted from the principalship of one of the Newark
grammar schools to organize the industrial schools
of that city. When the public high school was established he was unanimously selected to preside
over it, as afterward also over the city Normal
School.

"At this first meeting it was resolved to offer a
premium for the best essay on 'The necessity and
means of advancing the interest of common school
education in New Jersey.' The State Superintendent
laid a double eagle on the table, and the prize was
in due season awarded to Mr. Clark, the vice-president. The committee of award consisted of the president, the recording secretary, and Dr. Christopher
Columbus Hoagland.

"To this man, (Dr. Hoagland) more than any
other person, is due the whole educational movement
at the middle of the last century of which the founding of this association was so important a part.
Like the great discoverer whose name he bore, he
showed the way to a new world in which his fondest
ideals have been more than realized.

"When I first knew him in 1839, he had already
abandoned the medical profession to become a
teacher in Hunterdon county; but, the next year, he
returned to his native Somerset, where for more
than a dozen years he was town superintendent and
county examiner. In private and in public, in school-

An early picture of Bayard Street School, New Brunswick, where NJEA was founded.

houses and in other places of assembly, wherever and whenever he could get a hearing, his voice was heard in behalf of popular education. Without assumption of superiority, discouraged by no rebuff and disheartened by no failure, triumphing over even his own errors and weaknesses, he persisted until the people could not but hear and help."

THE EARLY YEARS

It was not until its eighth meeting, in Newark, April 1, 1862, that a motion authorized the Secretary (S. A. Farrand of Essex County) "to procure a suitable book for the records." The book thus procured is in the safe of the Association headquarters now. It starts with the constitution that was adopted at the 1853 meeting and with the signatures of the teachers who attended the ninth meeting at Bridgeton in December of 1862. G. M. Hoag of Belvidere was the first to sign. What happened during the earliest years must be gathered from other sources.

The question which most concerned the founders of the Association was the improvement of teaching. There were two approaches to it—the teachers institute for the benefit of teachers already in service, and a normal school to prepare their successors and future fellows.

THE INSTITUTES

The institutes came first. At the initial meeting, or shortly thereafter, Dr. Hoagland was designated "State Agent" of the new Association to advance the cause of teacher institutes.

"It was through his persistency," says Dr. Thompson, "that five teachers' institutes were held in Somerset before any were held elsewhere in New Jersey. During the year in which he held office, he succeeded in inducing the teachers of nine counties to attend teachers' institutes. When he removed to Illinois the association presented to him a watch with appropriate inscription."

Dr. Thompson was his successor.

JOHN BODINE THOMPSON

John Bodine Thompson is a fascinating character. His father, Joseph Thompson, superintendent in Readington Township, in 1852, held meetings on education in a grove in the center of the township. There, says his son,

"The Governor, the Attorney-General, the State Superintendent, and other men of influence who came and spoke words of encouragement, expressed the surprise they felt, as they drove through the country, at finding the farms and villages deserted.

On their return to Trenton they reported that they had spoken to seven thousand people. The newspapers published reports of the proceedings, and the influence spread abroad."

The son was born in 1830, near Pleasant Run, and graduated from Rutgers in 1851. He was only 23, therefore, when he helped found the Association, and 27 when he ceased his direct educational activities. He attended the Theological Seminary, and as Rev. John Bodine Thompson was a leading citizen of the State until his death in 1907. He retained his keen interest in schools, however, and in the Association. He made the main address at the 50th anniversary meeting, and his address to the pupils of Readington Township in 1899 is a classic defense of educational growth and the educational needs of rural areas.

H E WAS the Association's State Agent for two years (1855 and 1856), and his lengthy report on his work for teacher institutes appears as part of the report of State Superintendent Phillips for 1857. He says:

"The cardinal principle, which lies at the foundation of our educational system is, that 'A free people must be an educated people.' To promote these ends, it is necessary to have—

First, in the order of time, an appropriate place for teaching;

Secondly, pupils to be taught; and

Thirdly, a teacher able and loving to teach.

"The first and second of these—school-houses and the attendance of pupils—have been, measurably, attained; at least, the defects in these are, by universal consent, not so great as in the third particular. With wise discrimination, then, the New Jersey State Teachers' Association, since its first organization, whilst not neglecting these other so important particulars, has directed its efforts mainly towards securing throughout the State a corps of thoroughly qualified and efficient teachers. It has

justly considered this of the *first importance.* Nor
have these efforts been unsuccessful. On the contrary, notwithstanding the much that remains to be
done—and few among us have any conception of
how much that is—any one who will diligently com-
pare the present state of educational affairs in New
Jersey with that which existed when the N. J. State
Teachers' Association was organized, will plainly
perceive that the progress has been quite as great
as could consist with healthful development."

Describing his work, Mr. Thompson says: "Since
he entered upon the duties of his office he has com-
municated with teachers and people by means of
two thousand five hundred printed circulars, nine
hundred letters, one hundred public lectures (exclusive of the daily services of Teachers' Institutes)
given professional instruction to about thirteen hundred teachers, addressed thousands of children,
traveled more than ten thousand miles, in all sorts
of conveyances, over all sorts of roads, in all sorts
of weather; meeting with all sorts of receptions,
but with an earnest heart and a hopeful confidence
in his cause; never despairing, never doubting its
ultimate and speedy success, he has gone steadily
forward as best he could, and trusts that he has
not labored entirely in vain. The mode of procedure
has usually been to consult with some of the more
prominent teachers of a county respecting the arrangements for an Institute and induce them to call
a meeting of the teachers of the county, at which
the matter might be discussed, and some plan of
operations adopted. Where this was impracticable,
as was often the case, some one, usually a teacher
in the county, has been employed to visit the teachers at their schools, talk with them about the matter, and endeavor to secure their attendance at the
time and place indicated by a majority of those
consulted. Where county associations were in active
exercise, these preliminary arrangements have usually been entrusted to them."

"The Institutes which have been held under the
auspices of the N. J. State Teachers' Association,

were called to order at the time appointed, remarks were made respecting the design of our assembling, the important nature of our business, the necessity of proper preparation for that business, and the still greater necessity which exists that whoever undertakes to guide the workings of an immortal mind, must have the assistance of the Maker of that mind, who alone understands its mysterious mechanism. A portion of Scripture was then read, and the Divine guidance invoked. With such exercises the duties of each day began. After this, in order to dissipate that feeling of timidity which, while it exists, interferes so much with the success of the Institute, the members usually read some interesting article, designed, not for criticism, but that they might gradually acquire that self-confidence, so necessary to success in every undertaking. The necessity of unanimity of purpose in our exercises, the advantages of knowing each other, of feeling that we are members of the same profession, having a common interest, held together by a common bond of union, and other kindred topics, were then spoken of, after which a recess was announced, that the members might straightway begin to cultivate each others' acquaintaine, and the more speedily learn to feel themselves of the same family. The evenings were devoted to lectures and discussions, in which all present were requested to participate. Neither the catechetical nor the lecturiny system of instruction has been exclusively used."

STATE NORMAL

According to Mr. Thompson no mention was made of a normal school in the reports of the first meeting of the Association, "not because its importance was not recognized, nor because it was not fully and freely discussed; but because the time for it was not yet fully come. The people must first be educated up to see the necessity of it."

We have seen how Dr. Phillips, at the opening meeting, tossed a "double-eagle" on the table as the prize for the best essay on "The necessity and means of advancing the interest of common school education in New Jersey." The prize-winning essay by Mr. Clark was printed in the State-Gazette and was widely distributed in pamphlet form. Mr. Clark said:

"It has been thought that almost anybody could teach a common school; certainly those who could 'read, write, and cipher.' The fact that professional training is essential, must be understood and acknowledged—that not every person who has the requisite learning and ability, is 'apt to teach'—that not every person can govern himself, much less a school, forming in his pupils habits of order, habits which are as valuable as knowledge obtained from books—that teaching is both a science and an art— that it requires talents of the highest order—and that specific preparation is necessary as well in this as in any other profession or calling. . . .

"We must have, then, a State Normal School, with a Model School attached, wherein our young men and women shall be fitted for teaching, in the same manner as persons are fitted for other vocations, vis: by an apprenticeship, as a business for life."

At the Institutes held by Dr. Hoagland and Mr. Thompson, one of the evening lectures was always "in behalf of the normal school." As a result of this agitation, supported by such prominent citizens as Richard S. Field and David Naar, the Legislature in 1855, established the State Normal School, with an appropriation of $10,000 for its support. "Some enterprising citizens of Trenton" provided buildings for the accommodation of the institution, which was opened for students in March, 1856. At the same time Paul Farnum of Beverly contributed $70,000 in property and money for the founding of the Farnum Preparatory School in Beverly. For some time this served as an auxiliary department and training school for the Trenton institution.

With these major achievements to its credit in its

early years, the Association tended to rest on its laurels. Says Mr. Thompson: "The teachers were aroused and my services were not so much needed. No successor (as State Agent) was appointed. It was thought that without further stimulus there would be a steady pressing forward toward the ideals which had been evoked. This it seems was a mistake."

CIVIL WAR YEARS

The actual minutes of the Association, as we have noted, start in 1862. The Civil War was already begun, and many of the proceedings recall Association activities during other and later wars. The 1862 convention, for example, resolved: "that free schools are the only support, the only hope of free government, that popular education and popular liberty are inseparably related and must stand or fall together"; and "that the best interests of our Country require that all our educational institutions and appliances should notwithstanding the present unexampled drain upon our resources be continued and maintained."

Subsequent conventions debated the desirability of military instruction in our public schools, and favored the study of the constitution and our system of government in all schools.

The drafting of young men to war created, as it has done since, a teacher-shortage, especially acute because the proportion of men teachers was so high. When the Association was founded, men teachers outnumbered the women two to one. By 1861 State Superintendent Ricord was telling the Legislature:

"In the opinion of the township school officers females, as instructors, are quite as desirable as males; while as disciplinarians the preference is slightly in favor of males. . . . The notion that women cannot govern is overwhelmingly refuted by the experience of all ages. They were made to govern, and that too, by the only means by which government

FREDERICK WILLIAM RICORD

can be permanently maintained, namely by love, by
affection, by kindness . . . the 'great big boys', those
terrors of pedagoguedom, on whom schoolmasters
always look with trembling, speak to her in their
blandest terms, and, with their more solid acquirements, receive from her lessons of gentleness which
will give beauty and character to their future career.
But as all females are not beautiful, so all are not
amiable, and we must, both in our private and public
capacities, acquiesce in this mysterious arrangement
of Providence. Fortunately the chances are in our
favor, and schoolmistresses at $200 a year may,
without much hesitation, be selected in preference
to $300 schoolmasters."

A year later, for the first time, the women teachers outnumbered the men, 1108 to 1104. At the Bridgeton convention of the Association, in 1862, a committee of three was appointed "to report upon the comparative merits of males and females as teachers in the various departments of our common schools." For that committee, Mr. Betts, vice-principal of the Normal School, reported:

> "That notwithstanding woman's influence was felt and acknowledged to a certain extent, still there was a prejudice in some localities in reference to her adaptation to the work of instructing youth. He argued that women were in many respects peculiarly fitted. They are quicker, possess more intuition, have a better faculty of imparting information, are more ideal, less inclined to change, can adapt themselves particularly to the work of primary teaching as men cannot. He hinted at the difference made in pecuniary compensation, saying that men were in many instances better paid for doing a thing badly that women were for doing it well."

> The Association then resolved "that this Association is deeply impressed with the conviction of the superior adaptation of female teachers in the work of instruction and that we respectfully urge their claims upon the confidence of the school officers and friends of education throughout the State."

THIS CONVICTION of the superiority of female teachers was not carried into the operation of the Association, however. The original constitution (Art. II) had provided that "Any male teacher of the State of New Jersey having been proposed and elected may become a member of the association by signing this constitution. Each male member shall pay to the treasurer, the sum of one dollar annually. Any female teacher of the state may become a member by signing the constitution."

In 1864 this was amended to reduce the dues to $.50 and omit entirely any mention of the ladies. Not until 1873 were the "lady members" again recognized, by a resolution empowering the treasurer to "receive contributions" from them. Subsequently the dues of men again became a dollar, and in the great convention of 1886, the dues of "females" were set at $.50. Later, apparently in deference to the "lady members," dues were "equalized" at $.50, where they remained until 1921.

Women's intellectual contributions were valued more highly than their dues. In 1866 "Miss Chase of the Newark High School was invited to prepare an essay" for a meeting which was never held. In 1869 Mrs. Randall of the Oswego Training School (N. Y.), gave readings before the convention, and in 1870 Miss Rebecca Earles of Trenton read an essay on "Drawing as an Educator." In 1879 the Secretary thought it worthy of note that "Mrs. Ermine Smith of Jersey City joined in the discussion."

BROADENING THE CURRICULUM

During these years the principal and teachers of the State Normal School appeared regularly before the Association, which was steadfast in its support, expressing, in 1862 "our utter disapprobation of the attempts recently made to pull down these pillars in our educational fabric."

The curriculum was a topic of unending interest. A Mr. Berry of Rahway led the fundamentalists. He regularly introduced resolutions "that the State should educate her children as far as to enable them to read well, write well, and calculate well, and no further." These provoked sharp replies from such stalwarts as Peckham and the aged Nathan Hedges.

The Association sought guidance in the curriculum, designating a committee to report "upon a course of study best suited to the objects of our public schools."

For that committee, Prof. Phelps, head of the Normal School, reported "that they have consulted with the most prominent educators in the country, and their conclusion is, that what is wanted is a well defined *policy*. Only one State (Mass.) prescribes a course of study; in all other States the pupil is his own chooser of books, and the curriculum embraces the range of the sciences.

"The great principle is still unlearned, that the method is more important than the study taught."

Two years later, the committee still at work, concluded: "that no one course of study can be presented to be universally adopted and successfully followed everywhere and under all circumstances."

The advocates of a broadened curriculum clearly had the best of it. Natural history, object teaching, moral instruction, political instruction, education of the "whole man," geology, short methods in arithmetic were frequent topics of speechs and resolutions. In 1868, at Moorestown, W. A. Barringer of Newark, urged teachers "to proceed from the known to the unknown, from the concrete to the abstract, and never to do for a child what he can do for himself. The word method, combined with phonics, is best," he said, "for teaching the alphabet."

EARLY CONVENTIONS

It is a mistake to think of the Association meetings in those early days in terms of our modern conventions. An attendance of 50-75 seems to have been normal until late in the century. At the 50th anniversary meeting, James M. Green recalled:

"It was then the custom of the State Teachers' Association to move about. The theory was that bringing such an active, energetic and attractive company of people into a community and spreading them about—boarding around—would stir up something of educational enthusiasm; and it was quite the custom to go to a place and meet until we sort of wore the place out. The uniform experience was that we would have a largely increased attendance the first year. We might hold that attendance for two or three years; then it would begin to drop off a little as perhaps teachers came to feel that they knew that place pretty well; then we would take up our tents and move on.

"The State Association came to Long Branch in I think, 1878. I think they held about four meetings there at that time; and it was my duty to go about and find places where they were willing to board teachers at a dollar a day for five or six in a room. Our hotels took a part and gave us reduced rates for those who felt that they would like to visit them."

W ITH RARE EXCEPTION the Association continued to meet during Christmas Week, despite the handicaps of weather. In 1865, when it convened at Hacketts-town, Dr. John S. Hart, principal of the Normal School, moved that, "in view of the disagreeable state of the weather at this season of the year—it having stormed during the sessions of the Association for three con-secutive meetings—that the next meeting be held either in the month of July or August."

His motion was ineffective, however. The Executive Committee decided to postpone the 1866 meeting until winter "after the meeting of the Legislature." Eventually it was abandoned altogether, "failing to secure speak-ers and a suitable place for the meeting." The Associa-tion finally convened again in December 1867 at Plain-field, despite the absence of State Superintendent Apgar, who, the Secretary notes, had "a scriptural excuse for non-attendance, 'I have married a wife and therefore I cannot come.'"

THE ASSOCIATION, in those days, steered a close course in its relationship to the State Superintendent and the State Government. Once the State Superintendency was established as a professional, full-time position, most holders of that position were presidents of the State Association. Mr. Ricord and Mr. Harrison, and later Dr. Addison Poland seem to have moved from the Presidency into the State Superintendency. At the same time the Association retained its freedom from state control. Suggestions that the State contribute to the support of the Association ($100 was the figure) were vetoed by the Association itself.

In 1869, at a Morristown meeting, the town superintendents met with the State Superintendent two hours before the time designated for the Association to convene. Their action appears to have provoked criticism. Mr. Sears offered a resolution "that in our judgment the objections urged against the actions of Superintendents or of persons not actually engaged in teaching are constitutionally taken and that such honorary members are neither entitled to vote nor hold office in the State Teachers Association."

"FREE" SCHOOLS

This early period in the life of the Association culminates in a complete revision of the school law and the establishment of a state-wide system of free public schools by constitutional amendment.

As early as 1862 State Superintendent Ricord appeared before the Bridgeton meeting with "a paper on school laws of New Jersey . . . pointing out the existing defects which need correction." The Association was so impressed that it asked that he repeat his lecture to the two houses of the Legislature at its approaching session, and the President appointed a committee of three to make the necessary arrangements.

Mr. Ricord's successor, C. M. Harrison, continued to press for revision of the school law, and outlined the need for county superintendents, and their proposed duties. The 1865 convention set up a committee to "memorialize the Legislature in reference to revision of the school law,—particularly the clause restricting the amount of school money to be raised by townships for the support of schools to $3 per scholar."

As a result of these efforts the Legislature in 1866 created the State Board of Education and repealed the law permitting the use of state funds for sectarian schools. The following year it made further revisions, creating the county superintendency, and state, county, and local boards of examiners. It also forbad corporal punishment in New Jersey schools.

This last provision was the subject of heated discussion among the teachers in their association. In 1867 the Association by "almost unanimous" resolution asked that this clause be expunged from the law. A year later, after a speaker told the convention that "our youths are too rude, too contentious of superiors," there was a full-dress discussion of the problem. The Secretary reports:

> "Although quite a number expressed themselves in favor of this section as it had compelled teachers to look for other and better modes of punishment, still it was generally admitted that the law was wholly disregarded in many parts of the State. It was noted that of the *teachers* who spoke upon the question a majority were opposed to this part of the law."

For several years thereafter, conventions featured speeches on such topics as "School government," "Good order in our schools and the means by which it may be secured," and "The True Principles of Discipline."

The Lyons Farm Schoolhouse in Newark was long an historic landmark. Eventually it was transported, stone by stone, to the garden of the Newark Museum. This historic old photograph is from the files of the Newark Library.

By 1869 Superintendent Ellis A. Apgar, at the beginning of his long tenure in that office, recommended that all public schools be made free. At that time 739 were free and 578 were still supported in part at least by rate bills. Two years later, in a comprehensive revision of the State school law, free schools were established and a two mill tax was fixed for their support. The State School Fund was to get the money from the sale of riparian rights, a nine months school term was fixed, and the act to encourage school libraries was passed.

It remained to consolidate the gains in the form of constitutional amendments. This was achieved in 1875, when the State accepted, as part of its basic law, the provision that "The Legislature shall provide for the maintenance and support of a thorough and efficient system of free public schools for the instruction of all the children in this State between the ages of five and eighteen years." At the same time the Constitution was amended to settle, once and for all, the question of using public funds for sectarian or non-public schools.

There is little evidence of the part the Association played in these developments. We can only conclude that the issues were placed before the Association in such papers as Superintendent Apgar's 1869 address on "The Progress of Education in our State" and his 1875 speech on "The Separation of Church and School Interests."

T HE ATTAINMENT of free schools brought the question of attendance. In 1870 a committee was set up "to urge upon the Legislature the propriety and the great necessity of Legislative enactments to secure the attendance upon the schools of all children of school age in the State."

In 1873, "A delegation from the Organized Trades and Labor Unions of the State of New Jersey waited upon the Association and desired through its representative, Mr. M. L. Frost of Newark, recognition from this body of their efforts to secure the passage through the next Legislature of a Compulsory School Law."

Teacher-certification was a recurring problem through the third quarter of the 19th century. The teachers rebelled at certification by examination, and the Association urged that New Jersey—then as now a receiving-state for teachers—recognize the certification of other States. There was growing dissatisfaction with the teacher institutes, culminating in attempts to have the Association go on record for a normal school in each congressional district. Another problem which has a familiar ring was the compensation of the State Superintendent.

Among the topics of convention addresses and resolutions in these years were Natural History (does it lead to scepticism?); School Buildings and School Furniture; separation of the sexes; the kindergarten, The Relations of Conservatism and Radicalism to Education; spelling reform, the metric system (a hobby of Supt. Apgar); Froebel; the "child mind," high schools, grading, and hygiene.

At Long Branch in 1881 Henry Ward Beecher addressed the Association:

> "He earnestly advocated the building and thoroughly equipping of schoolhouses which should be equal in elegance and comfort to the best private residences of the sections in which they were located, and furnish them with instructors fitted by natural endowment and long training for their important work. Then pay them at least what their talents would command in other professions."

Elizabeth A. Allen

and

The Middle Years

Organizations, like individuals, rarely change overnight. The yeast of discontent obviously was working in the New Jersey State Teachers Association long before 1886. But on the surface the annual meeting of the Association at Trenton in Christmas Week of that year starts a new era. Certainly this was a major convention in the history of the NJEA.

While the general tone of the Association in the 70's was essentially professional and conservative, there were some indications that the teachers were considering what a stronger association might do. As early as 1865 Robert H. DeHart of Hackettstown listed as "means to the end of making teaching take rank among the other professions," 1. More perfect legal protection. 2. More perfect organizations. 3. More harmonious action. Committees were set up in 1877 to consider a "seaside home" for vacations and the idea of a Teachers' Life Insurance Association. Nothing came of either proposal, though a Mr. Bradley offered a large lot at the shore if the teachers would form a company and erect a suitable building. The building was estimated to cost $9,334, and its furnishings $1800.

Almost before President Charles E. Meleney of Paterson had called the 1886 Convention to order, there was a move to revise the constitution. In his own ad-

dress President Meleney looked to the future: He made
the following recommendations:

"That the association be established on a more
permanent basis; members should be elected; every
teacher should be a member; that the association
be more representative; county associations should
send delegates to the state teachers' association;
there should be a stronger union throughout the
state; positions would be more permanent and salaries more equable; teachers should rise to a higher
standard of excellence and demand proportionate
compensation."

He also proposed a state council of education composed of eminent educators, "to legislate upon educational matters and recommend to the state authorities
measures bearing upon school questions."

"Some of the subjects to be considered by the
council include the present condition of school
discipline; the result of the law prohibiting corporal
punishment; what to do with truants and incorrigi-
ble pupils; what is our duty as educators to the
untaught vagrants; what can be done to enlighten
communities on school matters, and convince them
of our needs; what legislation should be enacted
in regard to compulsory education and child labor,
or how may the present laws be more effectively
enforced; what is the best method of obtaining
school boards; what would be the effect of appointing women on school boards; what is the best
method of conducting teachers' examinations and
granting certificates; to what extent should temperance be taught; is it not important to teach the importance of labor; should not more attention be
given to instruction in the principles of our government."

Before the Convention ended, it set up a Committee
on Educational Progress, agreed to the dropping of non-
dues-paying members, and approved the idea of a State
Council of Education. The Committee on Educational
Progress was to have many of the functions of the
Association's present legislative committee, with the

Page 54

ELIZABETH A. ALLEN

President Stover and Executive Secretary Hipp look at old minute books.

added duty of framing broad legislative policy for the Association. This convention's program included speeches by E. A. Winship and Colonel Francis Parker (on Delsarte), and an address on "sub-primary" education.

The new vigor showed itself in all directions over the next few years. The Council of Education was set up, with half the members named by the Association and half by the Council itself. At the 1887 meeting there were exhibits (of Kindergarten and industrial arts), apparently for the first time. Resolutions urged an increase in the State tax, and demanded at least three years practical experience for county superintendents. The year's expenditures went over $100.

In another year the Educational Progress Committee —the first "permanent" committee of an association which eventually came to work largely through such committees—was able to report that the school tax had been increased to $5 per child, and desired changes had been made in certification. In 1888 the Association for the first time broke up into departmental meetings. In the mornings of convention days, superintendents and principals, grammar and high school teachers, and the primary teachers met separately. The departmental idea won favor; an attempt to abolish it was voted down the following year, and the Association, by resolution, held up the idea of *all* teachers as members.

INCORPORATION

For the next few years the yeast worked vigorously. Income from dues jumped substantially each year: $446.50 in 1889; $643.08 in 1890; and over $1,000 in 1895. The constitution was revised in 1890, though the revision—with peculiar provisions under which the President named three members of the Executive Committee —was relatively undemocratic and not destined for long use. Efforts were made to send the proceedings to members. The Educational Progress Committee—with Nicholas Murray Butler as its chairman in 1894—alerted the teachers to a variety of topics; suitable and sanitary buildings; high school facilities in rural areas; higher salaries for rural and primary teachers; compulsory education ("the present law is a dead letter"); improved supervision, manual training, kindergartens, and consolidation of districts.

In 1891 the Association met at Asbury Park, where meetings had to be moved out of Educational Hall when rain on the tin roof made hearing and speaking "difficult." Nevertheless it heard a paper on the Township versus the District system of organizing schools which made such a profound impression that its proposals were enthusiastically endorsed, and were enacted into law two years later—only to be substantially watered down by succeeding legislatures.

In 1893 the Association held no meeting on account of the Columbian Exposition, and its president, Dr. A. B. Poland, stepped into the State Superintendency. In 1896—its 43rd year—it took steps to incorporate. It met for that purpose in the Assembly rooms of the State Normal School at Trenton at 3:45 P. M. on Monday, December 28. The seal—the Association's name about the State Coat of Arms—read 1886, and had to be redrawn several years later.

E VEN BEFORE THIS, however, the Association had be-gun its activities in the major fields that were to occupy it for the next quarter-century. These were, of course, retirement, tenure, and minimum salary—and growing out of them, a vigorous program of legal defense of teachers whose rights as teachers were threatened.

Meeting at Asbury Park in July 1895, members received a 24-page printed report from the Committee on Educational Progress; S. E. Manness of Camden was its chairman. This report contained a discussion of Pensions. In it Mr. Manness meets two major criticisms of retirement plans, and hints at the joint-contributory plan which was finally to be adopted in 1919. He says:

"It has been argued that if we urge the adoption of pension legislation and possibly succeed, it will be followed by a reaction that will materially reduce the present salary list. Such has not been the experience in the past. The adoption of any legislation of that kind in this country fails to reveal a single instance where it was followed by a general reduction of the salary of the class receiving the benefit, or to be benefited by the proposed law. Again it is contrary to economic conditions; by relieving the teacher of anxiety in regard to the years when he shall have to yield his position to one younger, he is left free to devote his time and talents more enthusiastically to his work; result, greater efficiency, and hence more satisfaction on the part of his or her employers, and a willingness to increase rather than diminish salaries.

"Again it is argued that we expend our energies in securing an increase in salaries, and thus enable ourselves to become our own pensioners. To any possible or probable increase of the nature we are all willing, but the tendency now seems to be in the direction of lowering rather than increasing the emoluments in all official and semi-official positions, and while there is as yet no apparent movement of this kind against teachers, it is doubtful if any is possible in the way of increase.

"Now as to the plans for pensioning. There seems to me two plans feasible, *first*, the Philadelphia plan, which is essentially cooperation aided by donations until a fund has been obtained sufficient to yield an income adequate to the demands upon it; and *second*, the legislative plan, which aims to secure the enactment of laws establishing a fund and directing the application of the income to the pensioning of those who shall have reached the limit fixed upon for retirement, but not making it obligatory for any one to accept its provisions. Either of these plans might be successfully secured if the whole body of teachers were united in their action. Perhaps a plan uniting the two mentioned, whereby all teachers in the State were required to contribute a small percentage of their salaries on condition that the State appropriated a like sum each year, might be adopted."

ELIZABETH A. ALLEN

A year later as President Mr. Manness appointed an Association committee on Teachers Pensions. In this committee was developed the idea of a teacher-supported retirement fund administered by the State. The law creating this passed the legislature that same year.

It is impossible in this history of the Association to tell the detailed history of the retirement movements. The pension legislation was largely, however, the work of one person, Elizabeth A. Allen, the great teacher-

ELIZABETH A. ALLEN

leader of the next two decades, and one of the great teacher-leaders of all time. Born about the time the Association was being founded, she was graduated from Trenton Normal and began to teach at a very early age in Atlantic County. In 1871 she was employed at Hoboken. She must have been a dynamic character even then, since she was vice-president of the Association in the eighties, while still under 30.

Miss Allen's own interest in teacher retirement began in 1890. With two other Hoboken teachers she developed pension proposals which came before the legislature in 1891, 1893, 1894, and 1895. Money for their campaigns came first from their own pockets and then from teachers in Hoboken, Jersey City, Newark, Bayonne and other cities. Eventually she turned to the Association for help, with the results we have seen.

W ITH THE Teachers Retirement Fund created, Miss Allen was concerned with forging, from the Association, an instrument for its promotion and protection. To this end she needed to change the structure of the Association. An 1897 attempt to upset the process of appointing Association officers and secure election from the floor lost by a 75-81 vote. However, a committee was appointed to revise the constitution, though there were no women on it.

The 1898 convention, when this committee reported, brought an internal struggle which makes later ones seem tame indeed. At midnight, before the convention opened, the committee had approved only minor revisions. By the following morning, however, two members of the committee withdrew their signatures from the majority report, and submitted minority recommendations for an enlarged, elected nominating committee, with guaranteed representation on it for women. On a test vote on the Convention floor, Miss Allen won 167-102. The new constitution eliminated the old requirements for election to membership and provided that only those engaged in supervision or teaching might vote.

In a final compromise W. L. R. Haven of Morristown, leader of her opponents, was made President of the Association, while Franklin Thorn of Paterson, male leader of Miss Allen's forces, became head of the new Retirement Fund Department. The scars of the battle remained, however. During the following year two of the elected officers resigned. Bitter contests marked the election of officers in 1899 and 1900, and the "new" constitution was again revised—into the essential form which was to last, with minor amendments, for a whole generation. In this revision the Association failed to provide for election of its representatives on the Council of Education, which thereafter continued as an independent organization.

THE TEACHERS' CONGRESS

By 1900, however, Miss Allen's group seems to have been in control of the Association. She herself was secretary of the Teachers Retirement Fund, a member of its board of Trustees and of various Association committees. She herself addressed the 1900 Convention, and her speech, "The Teachers' Congress" set the objectives for the years ahead. This was a major speech in the history of the Association. In it, she said:

"The annual meeting of the State Teachers' Association should be the teachers' congress, the teachers' parliament, where might be freely discussed all matters that concern the interests of the teachers and the schools. In my opinion the one Teachers Association of the State had, in these respects, failed of its duty and its privilege. Its one yearly meeting seemed to be organized chiefly as a school of pedagogy, and with little or no reference to questions of vital moment to the teachers, the schools, the children and the taxpayers of our Commonwealth . . . A year ago much fear was expressed lest controversial questions be introduced in our meeting . . . The highest ambition of our Association should be to make its annual meeting controversial. It should be the assembly where the voice of the teacher shall be heard regarding all matters concerning the teachers and the schools, and where such questions shall be fully considered and debated.

"Among the subjects that materially affect teachers are those of examinations and certificates, tenure of office and transfers, salaries, and the question of what may properly be expected of teachers in the way of work and study outside of school hours.

"Teachers are said to lack 'esprit de corps.' We shall always lack 'esprit de corps,' so long as we have no professional ethics, no standards of courtesy and duty toward one another as teachers, and feel no responsibility for each other's conduct and welfare . . . You cannot treat the teachers like slaves without bringing up a race of slaves. Let me say to you, my fellow teachers, if you stand by and see injustice perpetrated upon your comrades and do not raise a note of protest, you get your just desserts if the next blow falls upon you. An injury to the humblest teacher in the State should be specifically resented by an official protest from this Association."

THE OBJECTS Miss Allen set forth became the objectives of the Association. To make them effective, however, there were further changes in the Association and its method of work. The Executive Committee—which had met only rarely to plan the convention—began to hold monthly meetings—often in New York City. It arranged to keep minutes, and authorized the secretary to employ a stenographer and a typewriter for that purpose. The Association directed that the Treasurer be bonded, and voted compensation of $50 a year for both the Treasurer and the Secretary.

Speakers from other states were brought to the convention to speak on legislative matters, notably Margaret Haley of Chicago and Thomas Hunter of New York City. Mr. Hunter said, "I would urge upon you to think and toil by day and night, to agitate, to importune, to see the legislators individually, to appoint committees

WILLIAM N. BARRINGER, Newark Superintendent and a vigorous nineteenth century Association leader.

to interview the leading men of the State. Be prepared with your arguments. Be sure you are right. Be courageous and fear not."

Especially important to the broader objectives was greater enrollment in the Association. For this task Powell G. Fithian of Camden was selected. A director

Page 63

of music, and himself a popular baritone soloist and song leader at conventions, Mr. Fithian brought phenomenal determination and enthusiasm to the task of making every New Jersey teacher an Association member. In his initial report he said:

"When we stop to consider what this Association is endeavoring to do for all public school teachers, we cannot easily understand why any teacher can refuse to join it. Surely no legislative body would be so foolish as to enact legislation for any body of people, when it was clearly shown that a bare majority of its members desired such legislation. We have no way of determining what the teachers of this State desire, unless they subscribe to an organization whose principle may be clearly defined. We feel quite sure, that from time to time, as we secure those things so essential to us as teachers, and for which we are, and have been so long striving, viz. tenure of office, minimum salary, pension laws, etc. that there is no one, whether he belongs to the Association or not, who will not always be willing to bear his cross, and accept with grateful heart all that comes his way . . . This committee is a unit in the belief, that every teacher in the State, who is eligible to membership in this Association, should be a member of it, and that our duty as members does not end, until we have used every honest effort we can make for the accomplishment of that end."

In his first year Mr. Fithian's committee enrolled 3,326 members out of some 9,157 teachers in the State. Then, as now, enrollment was highest in some of the rural counties, notably Atlantic, Camden, and Gloucester. By 1920, when these middle years end, Mr. Fithian was still chairman of the Enrollment Committee, and had enrolled as members of the Association 16,121 out of a potential 18,177 teachers—nearly 90 percent.

PENSION IMPROVEMENTS

The creation of the Teachers Retirement Fund did not end the desire of the teachers for greater state participation in their old-age security. A major source of controversy was the cost of administering the Fund. While the law placed the responsibility of administration on the State, a ruling by the Attorney-General made the Fund itself liable for administrative costs. The teachers sought legislation to change this and recover the money already paid out for this purpose. Governor Voorhees, however, was unfriendly as a result of circulars distributed during his election campaign, for which the Association was blamed. Twice he vetoed bills passed by the Legislature to have the State assume the costs of administration. In 1904 Governor Stokes, a former superintendent in Millville, took office and promptly signed the desired legislation.

Governor Voorhees, had, however, approved a measure that was to have far-reaching effects on teacher-thinking about retirement. This was the Teachers Half-Pay Pension Law, which said simply:

"Any school teacher in this state, who shall have served as such in any school district of this state for forty (40) years consecutively, shall, upon application to the board having charge of the schools in such district, be voluntarily retired from active duty upon half-pay; and it shall be the duty of the body having charge of the finances of said district to provide for such payment monthly."

This was not an Association-sponsored measure. As told by John Enright in 1917:

"Mr. Linsley was principal of School No. 1 in Jersey City. He did his work so well with the boys that when they got in the Legislature, and got to be Governors of the State, they remembered their old schoolmaster. He had then grown aged, and the members of the Legislature from Hudson County introduced a bill providing for a pension to all teachers who had served for a period of forty years in one place . . . It was special legislation, of course, in general terms conforming with the Constitution of the State as to legislation. Mr. Linsley, like every true man, no matter what his years, arose to the full height of his stature and said; 'I am not an old man. I will not accept your pension,' and he continued as a teacher for several years after the pension had been provided for him, thus setting a splendid example that has prevailed ever since."

Miss Allen was critical of this legislation as benefitting only "that very limited number of fortunate teachers whose 'lines have fallen in pleasant places.'" There were soon others to point out that aged teachers who qualified under both retirement plans could spend their declining years "very comfortably" on more than their working salary, and others who agitated for a reduction of the 40-year requirement and liberalization of its consecutive employment requirements. This was achieved in 1906, and the idea of 35-years service became deeply ingrained into New Jersey teachers.

The third major problem in teacher retirement was the insecurity of the retirement system itself unless membership in it was made compulsory. This was achieved by a general revision of the Retirement Fund law also in 1906. Rates for the older members were increased and all teachers entering service after January 1, 1908 were required to become members.

SALARIES, TENURE

At the 1902 Convention, William Rabenort of Paterson introduced a resolution to consider the advisability of establishing a minimum salary in the public schools of New Jersey and the wisest means of preventing any reduction of the salaries paid in such schools. A committee was promptly appointed, which agreed to call itself the Committee on Teachers Salaries. It resolved in favor of a $450 minimum and "to seek protection that salaries shall not be reduced during employment."

By the time it reported—in 1903—it had become the Special Committee on Teachers Salaries and Tenure of Office. Its chairman, H. Budd Howell of Phillipsburg was a vigorous fighter for the rural areas. Later he was

ADDISON B. POLAND, State Superintendent, New-ark Superintendent, and Association President.

to stand before the Association and say, "I am afraid that in this Association, which is, of course, more or less dominated by the city teacher . . . there is a disposition to forget to redeem certain promises that have been made by this Association to the rural teacher

. . . I have not seen the slightest disposition to do anything primarily for the country teacher."

In his 1903 report, however, Mr. Howell presented a factual study of salaries and tenure, both in New Jersey and nation-wide. He showed that average salaries ranged from $52.52 a month for men in Sussex and $36.81 for women in Warren County, to $170.22 for men in Hudson and $66.77 for women in Essex. He also showed that there were districts with average salaries of $25.56 a month for men and $24.00 a month for women. He noted that

"In 28 cities and towns of New Jersey the lowest annual salary ranges from $350 to $575, with two exceptions where the lowest salaries are $300 and $315; eight pay beginners about $400; seven about $450; and six about $500."

His survey showed Pennsylvania, Indiana and West Virginia with some form of minimum salary laws (Penna. was $35 a month) and Massachusetts, New York and Montana with forms of tenure acts. He gathered opinions on the minimum salary law, finding 10 county superintendents in favor, five opposed and two non-committal. Of 28 superintendents and principals, 16 were in favor, eight opposed, and four non-committal. One of the objections has been heard regularly ever since. Said his correspondent: "The minimum if made, would at once fix in the minds of the average board of education that sum as the amount fixed by law as the pay of all teachers. They would regard it as not only minimum but also maximum."

SUCH ARGUMENTS against the minimum salary proposal proved strong enough to prevent united Association support at that time. Legislation was not actually passed until 1919. The interest of the committee and of the Association directed itself toward tenure instead. Lydia K. Ennis and other members of the Jersey City Teachers' Club had the first bill drafted, and submitted to Miss Allen.

While the original concept was merely to prevent re-
ductions in salary, the bill Mr. Hudspeth introduced
into the legislature in 1904 is remarkably similar to the
law on the books today. It said:

"No principal or teacher shall be removed or
dismissed or reduced in salary or grade by any
board of education, except for just cause, and after
written charge or charges of the cause or causes of
complaint shall have been preferred . . . signed by
the person or persons making such charge or charges,
and filed with the secretary or clerk of said board,
and after the said charge or charges have been
publicly examined into by the board of education
upon such reasonable notice to the person charged
and in such manner of examination as the rules
and regulations governing the same may prescribe,
it being the intent hereof to give every principal
and teacher against whom charges for any cause
may be preferred, a fair trial upon such charges
and every reasonable opportunity to make defense."

The tenure idea was opposed by the State Board of
Education, the State Department, and many superintendents working through the Council of Education. Nevertheless, year after year the Association pressed for the
legislation. Legislative Chairman E. C. Mackey of Trenton said: "Year by year, the teacher is acquiring an increasing vested interest in and right to her position, and
a potential annuity of which she should not be deprived
except for a just and adequate cause and by due process
of law. The teacher has now a more equitable, legitimate
and urgent claim upon the State for protection against
arbitrary dismissal from service and reduction of salary
. . . We believe that a proper tenure of office has really
found a place in the unwritten Bill of Rights, and that
the opportune time has come for it to be made a matter
of record."

He was not far wrong. In 1908 the bill passed the
Senate, after a campaign in which Association members
wrote "thousands of letters" and distributed over 10,000
circulars. It failed in the Assembly, however, by four

votes. The defeat was followed by further conferences
between representatives of the Association, the Council,
the State Department and the State Board. A temporary
compromise was reached on a proposal that included
superintendents, but did not provide for written charges
against the teachers. Finally, in 1909, it was agreed to
drop the superintendents out of the bill, include the
written charges, and pass it—as many tenure bills have
been passed since—to take effect the following September, giving boards the opportunity to dismiss teachers
they did not want to employ permanently.

T HE POSSIBILITY that thousands of teachers would be
thus dismissed caused consternation, even amongst the
most vigorous supporters of the bill. The Executive
Committee promptly retained Joseph Tumulty of Jersey
City as counsel and four other lawyers "for the defense."
It called a special meeting of the Association in Elks
Hall, Jersey City on May 29, 1909, at which, after re-
placing a lost overcoat of a Mr. Moore, it was resolved:

"That with freedom from anxieties incident to an
uncertain tenure, and with professional rights pro-
tected by law, we pledge ourselves to increased de-
votion and undivided attention to the best interests
of the Public Schools.

"That the Association does not stand for the defense of incompetence or inefficient teachers, or for
any interference with Boards of Education in the
performance of their manifest duties; but it does
deprecate the dismissal of efficient teachers without a hearing and without just cause, especially
those who are nearing the time of retirement.

"That the Association approves the action of the
Executive Committee in the employment of legal
counsel and authorizes the Committee to make such
further expenditure for this purpose as may be
necessary."

Apparently the number of dismissals was nowhere
near so great as had been feared; the threats, however,
intensified the Association's determination to protect,

at any cost, the advance it had made. Out of this grew the Grievances and Redress Committee (now Welfare) for the legal protection of teachers and their interests.

While the teachers were so greatly concerned with pensions and tenure, other important changes were taking place in the educational scene. In most of these the Association took a part, if not a leading role. Resolutions supported the building of a second normal school (Montclair), the spread of physical education, mandatory medical inspection of school pupils, special facilities for handicapped children, especially the mentally defective, working papers for children over 14, and increased financial support of education which took the form of dedicating to schools the income from the main stem railroad tax.

In 1904, at its Trenton meeting, the Convention observed the 50th anniversary of the Association with a whole evening of reminiscences. Dr. A. B. Poland, by that time the Newark Superintendent, looked forward as well. He said:

"We know the long fight over the curriculum—over the three R's and the fads. The so-called fads were with us a half century ago; they are with us still; and it is likely, they will be with us a half-century hence . . .

"In the next fifty years . . . we shall have buildings that not only conform to all the principles of sanitation, but that are likewise beautiful in external appearance. Besides the usual class room they will have a library, a gymnasium, a workshop—and possibly a bath."

Nor were the conventions lacking in solid professional values. Notable convention addresses came from John Cotton Dana, famed Newark librarian, and Woodrow Wilson, then President of Princeton. Mr. Dana, urging wider interest in school libraries, advanced an interesting theory concerning textbooks: "A book for school use may be too well made . . . The ideal school book is one that will fall apart about the point when it gets so dirty it wants to be burned."

Page 71

On "The State and the Citizen's Relation to it," President Wilson delivered one of his thoughtful, scholarly, wise addresses. He said:

"Nothing is a proper object of the State which cannot be embodied into law . . . The object of the State is not to express in written form handsome desires, but to put in workable shape certain imperative commands; and it is necessary, in order that we should do that, that these commands should have back of them our general agreement . . .

"We have boasted of political liberty. Political liberty will have gone out of the world when everybody shall have conformed. Political liberty is the apotheosis of insurgency. Political liberty is the negation of conformity. The men who kick over the traces are the men who keep political liberty alive; not the men who conform. The men who won't go with the organization are the men who save the organization itself, by reminding it that it must always square itself with principle or else lose the allegiance of those who try to square their lives and their hopes by principle."

TEACHER PROTECTION

With the tenure law safely passed and the retirement system compulsory came the problem of legal protection for these gains. The first of these rose in connection with the retirement fund. Several boards had failed to cooperate in making deductions from teachers' salaries for the Fund while membership was still voluntary. Passaic was one of the worst offenders and continued its refusal to make deductions when membership became compulsory.

In 1910 the Executive Committee—now holding its meetings in Atlantic City and noting with dismay the rising cost of speakers ($125 for G. Stanley Hall and $100 for Henry Van Dyke)—offered to cooperate with the Retirement Fund trustees "financially or otherwise in all efforts they may make to defend the constitutionality of the Retirement Fund act." A Passaic teacher,

ELIZABETH A. ALLEN

Myrtle Allen, brought a test case; the Retirement Fund itself raised over $1700 by contributions, and in February 1911 the Supreme Court upheld the Retirement Fund act.

P OWELL G. FITHIAN was now President of the Association, and at the 1911 convention he discussed the question of all legal protection of teacher rights:

"Recognizing the fact that unscrupulous Boards might take advantage of the defenseless teacher, this Association long since took steps to secure for her the protection of law. It was active in securing the passage of several laws of great benefit to the whole teaching body; so far, however, as actually defending a teacher when unjustly accused or deprived of her rights under the law, the Constitution and By-laws of this Association make no provision whatever. Nevertheless I have always maintained that the Association should take cognizance of these matters. Do not infer from this that it should belittle itself by petty officiousness or lessen its influence by the stand that a member must always be right. Clearly there can be no judicious action taken without a knowledge of the absolute facts in each case. This calls for an investigation which should be earnest, thorough and impartial, seeking only to establish truth. If the results show that the teacher has been assailed in her inalienable rights under the law—has been wronged—and that justice has been trampled under foot, then the Association should throw down the gauntlet and accept the challenge. It should assume the defense of the teacher whom even a statute of the State does not protect. It should use all possible means to secure justice. There should be no doubt, no apathy, no half-heartedness in its procedures. That teacher's case today may be yours or mine tomorrow. No one is safe until the limitations and scope of the law in question have been defined."

Even more significantly, Elizabeth A. Allen again appeared before the Convention with an address again titled "The Teacher's Congress," to deal with the duty of the Association toward its members. She said:

"The whole is no greater than the sum of its separate parts. The good of one, is the good of all. The rights, privileges and immunities of its members must ever be the most sacred object of the Association, else its purpose is a failure. It must maintain unceasing vigil, and forever stand guard."

She detailed several specific cases:

Marcus Glazer of Flemington held a contract as a principal when Flemington Boro broke off from Raritan Township, and the new Flemington board refused to honor the contract. The Commissioner upheld the Board, the State Board reversed the decision, and the Supreme Court sided with the Commissioner. Thus far Mr. Glazer, a member of the Association's Enrollment Committee, had fought his own case. Miss Allen said, however, "The average teacher is utterly unable financially to prosecute or defend a suit. This Association is powerful financially and morally. It is its *duty*, it ought to be its *joy*, to fight the just battles of its members."

Sue H. Coles, supervising principal in Pilesgrove, refused to promote a high school pupil against the wishes of the Board, claiming that "promotion ought not to be made without the cooperation of the teachers." As the dispute became warm, the Board declared her position vacant. Eventually, in compliance with the tenure act, the Board filed charges. On appeal, Assistant Commissioner Betts upheld Miss Coles and she was reinstated.

Hower T. Marstellar, supervising principal in Pleasantville, had made himself unpopular in some quarters by his vigor in enforcing the truancy act. He took "three loaded revolvers of large calibre" away from boys on the school playground, and the parents of two of the boys became candidates for the board. He insisted that the railroad tax money be used to increase teachers salaries, establishing a minimum of $550. Apparently on his advice the Board refused to pay tuition to Atlantic City high school for a pupil lured there for his baseball prowess; the pupil's father became president of the Pleasantville board.

The Board, ignoring the tenure act, elected a successor to Mr. Marstellar, was stopped by a court order, declared his position vacant, was again reminded of the need of filing charges, tried to keep the schools closed through September so that Mr. Marstellar could not act, held secret meetings, etc. A libel suit by Mr. Marstellar caused a local editor to leave the state. Mr. Marstellar became superintendent at Salem, from which position he continued his fight.

The case of Elsie B. Nicholson of Swedesboro involved the right of a new board to accept a resignation already refused by their predecessors.

Miss Allen concluded:

"Suppose the Association should prosecute these cases and lose all of them, what benefit would result?

"1. Notice would be served on the occasional board of education which is disposed to deal unjustly with a teacher, that it must deal with this powerful association, and not with a financially helpless man or woman.

"2. Defeat in the courts would show weak places in the law, and enable us to proceed intelligently to remedy them.

"3. Such action, though resulting in temporary defeat, would unify and inspirit the teachers of New Jersey as nothing else has ever done.

"4. Such action would add thousands to the membership of this organization.

"5. It is wise and righteous for this Association to make its own, and fight to a finish, the case of any member who is oppressed and unjustly attacked in his or her professional capacity. This Association could have no more ideal motto than 'Bear ye one another's burdens'!"

The outcome of this meeting was the creation, at this same 1911 convention, of a Grievances and Redress Committee, of which Miss Allen was a key member. The members also adopted a series of resolutions urging the further strengthening of the tenure act, employment of counsel, investigation of the cases reported by Miss Allen, the drafting of a code of ethics, and clerical assistance for the president.

The new committee took immediate action. Within a year the Association had reimbursed Miss Coles with $271.05 for legal expenses; Miss Nicholson with $150, and Mr. Marstellar with $531.44. The Association carried Mr. Glazer's appeal to the Court of Errors and Appeals with Senators Feidler and Gebhardt as counsel. On still another case, involving the transfer of a principal to a teaching position, it paid fees of $980.

It also introduced, in at least two cases, the practice of conferences between Association representatives and board members. In one such case Miss Allen and Miss McNamara confered with the Atlantic City Board. When they asked to see a copy of the Board's resolution of dismissal, the Board members told them that "the blamed thing some one tried to paste on wouldn't stick." They note, however, the courtesy and amity of the conferences.

FIRST WOMAN PRESIDENT

On the wave of these achievements, Miss Allen became the first woman president of the State Association. She was not elected, however without a struggle. Her long years of Association work had made her many enemies. Teachers were beginning to realize that the Teachers' Retirement Fund, despite all her efforts, could not survive on the low contribution rates charged and pay the promised benefits to all the older teachers who had joined in its early years. Her administration of the Fund—somewhat dictatorial, perhaps, because it was *her* Fund—and not always business-like, since she was

more genius than bookkeeper, had been sharply criticized. At the annual meeting of the Fund in September
1913 a Miss McCoy of New Brunswick asked critical
questions, and a committee was appointed to investigate
the Fund. While the committee reported its conviction
"that the Fund is wisely. honestly, efficiently managed,"
Miss Allen obviously felt the need of justification which
election to the Presidency of the Association would
give. She was nominated and elected, and then, says the
secretary, "read from manuscript an appropriate in-
augural address."

"My election was thrust on me by my enemies . . .
I thank my enemies. I declare that, but for them.
nothing could have induced me to assume this great
responsibility, with the vast amount of work it
entails.

"It is asserted that this election will 'disrupt' the
Association; 'will put it back ten years.' . . . Is it
because the President-elect is a woman? Are not
the women entitled to at least *one* President in
Sixty years?

"It is asserted, too. as a matter of reproach and
danger, that 'Miss Allen controls the Association.'
May I ask,—in what way does Miss Allen control
the Association? What harmful policy has she ever
advocated? What unworthy man has she ever supported for office? . . . Our former Presidents, many
of them here, are requested, if I have not stated the
exact truth, to stand up and say so?"

In conclusion, however, she turned from the bitterness
and sounded the forward note that was characteristic
of her.

"I *will* not, I *cannot*, I *do* not believe that the
school men of New Jersey will not support my administration loyally and zealously.

"While we must 'make haste slowly', it should be
our immediate purpose to so amend the Thirty-Five
Years' Half-Pay Pension Act as to extend its bene-

fits to *all* of New Jersey's veteran teachers. We must guard our Retirement Fund from harmful, unwise or inopportune amendments. We must maintain inviolate the principles of our Tenure of Service Act. We must lend our influence and aid to every educational advance; we must raise the standard of excellence, and insist upon adequate remuneration for teachers. A minimum salary law should be secured as soon as expedient. It should be the aim of this Association, while preserving absolute independence, to cultivate close and friendly relations with the Department of Public Instruction, the State Board of Education, the local Boards of Education, and the various State and local organizations.

ONE PROJECT close to Miss Allen's heart came to fruition at that 1913 Convention. Assistant Commissioner A. B. Meredith brought to the Convention its first Code of Ethics. It was not greatly dissimilar to the code now in effect, though it has been revised repeatedly since then. Like the present code, it neither contained nor suggested any method of enforcement.

Also at this Convention, a committee composed of William A. Wetzel, James E. Bryan, and Frank H. Lloyd—originally asked to consider only the time and place of the annual meeting—brought in a report which discussed at length, though recommending against, a Delegate Assembly and voting by mail. They did suggest making independent nomination and constitutional amendments easier, and closer relations between the Association and local and county associations. The latter was much in mind, and the Association, by resolution asked that legislative information be sent local groups.

Two years later the proposed amendments were adopted, though an attempt by Miss Allen to increase dues to $1 for all members resulted only in cutting the men's dues to $.50.

ELIZABETH A. ALLEN

RETIREMENT CHANGES

Miss Allen's election as President, however, could not halt the inevitable. Pressure for the repeal of the tenure act and criticism of the retirement system continued. It must have worn down such leaders as Henry M. Maxson, long chairman of the legislative committee. In 1915, when the Federated Boards and teachers held a conference in mid-session of the Legislature, the teachers agreed to extend the probationary period of tenure from three to "five years and reemployment for a sixth." Other controversies arose, however, and the bill failed to pass. The Federated Boards were also seeking to amalgamate the Teachers Retirement Fund and the 35-year Pension plan, by that time a State rather than a local responsibility.

Miss Allen bitterly opposed both moves, and from the floor of the Convention forced through a resolution denouncing the "merging" of the retirement systems and the extension of the probationary period for tenure.

The line was held on tenure, but Miss Allen could not stop the changes in the retirement system. The Legislature appointed a commission under Assemblyman Arthur N. Pierson to investigate state pension systems. The battle in the Convention over cooperation with this commission was so bitter that Assistant Commissioner John Enright and his entire resolutions committee resigned in protest at remarks made by Arthur W. Milbury, Miss Allen's assistant secretary in the Retirement Fund office. A counter-motion to withdraw Mr. Milbury's honorary membership in the Association lost 54-53. Miss Allen had to be content with a memorial asking the Legislature to postpone action on teacher pension matters for one year.

A year later the Association was still divided and unready for decision. Another special committee on retirement plans had been appointed and served only to clarify the issues slightly. The great body of the teachers were recognizing the necessity of some changes, however, and in a contested election in 1917, Henry M. Cressman of Atlantic County, became President over E. A. Murphy of Jersey City, a staunch friend of Miss Allen. Alexander J. Glennie of Newark became vice-president. In the next generation, Essex and Mercer were to provide a larger share of the leadership.

The Pension and Retirement Fund Commission gradually formulated the law creating the present Teachers Pension and Annuity Fund. In 1918 Mr. Enright appeared before the Convention to explain its proposals. Even while cooperating with Mr. Pierson, he argued against the 62-year retirement age as too high, and he did secure the use of a five-year, rather than a ten-year period, for measuring final average salary. Exhausted by her struggles, Miss Allen was fatally ill, and unable to attend the convention. While paying deep tribute to her, the Association repealed its 1916 policy statement against the merging of Funds, and with this question apparently settled, turned its attention to new fields, passing resolutions in favor of an increased State School Tax, superintendents' tenure, and a $900 minimum salary. During the 1919 session of the Legislature, Mr. Glennie worked constantly in Trenton to secure amendments to the proposed bill which would be satisfactory to both the teachers and the Pierson Commission. On April 10, 1919, Governor Walter E. Edge signed the amended bill, which created the present Teachers' Pension and Annuity Fund.

Miss Allen's death, less than a month later, reminded the Association of all that it owed her, and brought forth a unique tribute. At a memorial session of the Convention, the speakers were Governor Edward C. Stokes, Judge James F. Minturn, and Mrs. Lucia Ames Mead. The Governor, especially, spoke at great length. He said:

> "For nearly a quarter of a century Miss Allen was the unchallenged leader of the New Jersey State Teachers' Association; not until she was on

her dying bed was she defeated, and today the vital principles of the Association are those she breathed into it."

By formal action on its closing day the Association adopted the following resolution:

"That this Association hereby elects Miss Elizabeth A. Allen as Honorary President of this Association *in perpetuam*, and that her name be printed hereafter in the reports of the Association."

MRS. STELLA S. APPLEGATE

The Modern Association

T HE YEAR 1920 closely resembles some recent years
—say 1948. A world war had ended only a few years
before. Automobiles, airplanes, movies and radio were
accepted features of living. Inflation had greatly shrunk
the purchasing power of teachers, and created hundreds
of local crises. There was an acute shortage of qualified
teachers.

The teachers had just been a party to the setting up
of an actuarial retirement system in which each teacher
—if it worked—would have a big stake, including substantial deposits of his own money. By the tenure act
and other legislative achievements, the Association had
demonstrated what it could do for the individuals who
made it up. A new and vigorous group of men had risen
to a position of leadership in the Association.

In 1919 President Alexander J. Glennie appointed
a special committee "to devise a plan to arouse the people of the State to a need of a better support of education." Under the leadership of James J. Hopkins of
Jersey City "a suite of offices in Newark was rented,
an expert 'drive' manager, expert publicity director and
force of clerks were placed in charge . . . subcommittees
were formed reaching into every township and borough."
Over $14,000 was raised by voluntary contributions from
the teaching force of the State, and over $12,000 spent.
The balance was finally turned over to the Association
for continued publicity activity.

OFFICE OF ADMINISTRATION

It was natural, too, to think of strengthening the Association, of ceasing to rely wholly on volunteer work-
ers. Other states were doing the same thing—Pennsylvania, in 1921, was the fourteenth to create the position

of Executive Secretary. There was agitation for a similar position in New Jersey. Dues were raised from $.50 to $1.00, and the question of a full-time secretary was referred to the Executive Committee, which subsequently reported in favor of it, but said it could not be done short of $2.00 dues. It proposed, instead, that the Association set up "an office of administration in Trenton."

"The purpose of an administrative office is to put the work of the Association on a business basis. The plan would require the employment of one clerk who would perform much of the detail work now done by the Secretary. She would gather information for Standing and Special committees. She would keep the files and records; issue bulletins of interest to the teachers; keep the local associations in touch with the State Association, etc.

"The plan of having a clerk, under the direction of the Executive Committee, would give the Association all the benefits of a well-knit, unified organization and, at the same time, avoid the commonly objectionable features involved in the plan of having a full-time secretary."

In APRIL 1923, the Executive Committee reports that it has opened an office in Room 304, Stacy Trent, and "a very competent person has been placed in charge." The Association was to remain in the Stacy Trent (in Room 307 and later in the 200 suite) until it moved to its own Headquarters Building in 1951. The "very competent person" was Mrs. Stella S. Applegate who was to remain a fixture in Association affairs until she retired in 1940.

CONVENTION DATES AND PLACES
As we have seen, it was customary in the early days to move the Association convention from place to place, and with some exceptions which did not turn out well, to hold it during Christmas Week. Dissatisfaction with meeting "on their own time" began as early as 1889, when a resolution asked the State Board to close schools

one Friday for the Association meeting. By 1920 this had become an issue; an "indignant citizen" was writing to the Newark Evening News to protest the use of school time for the convention.

Two years later, Ide G. Sargent proposed a bill which was, in essence, the law as it exists today, granting two days for convention attendance without loss of pay. His proposal became law in 1923, and the 1924 convention was held at the time which is now traditional—November 8-11.

The 1924 convention returned to Atlantic City after a two-year absence. Toward the end of the 19th century the convention had grown so large it could not be held in the smaller communities. For some years it alternated between Trenton and Newark, with Trenton having a distinct edge, because of the normal school facilities. In 1905, however, immediately after its 50th anniversary meeting, the convention moved to Atlantic City for the first time. There it stayed, despite protests from the teachers in the northern section of the State. In an effort to placate them, a few special meetings were held in Newark, but this was an unsatisfactory compromise. The Association voted to hold its 1922 meeting in Trenton, and in a bitter struggle there, agreed to go to Newark the following year. Thereafter it returned to the shore city, where it has continued to meet every year except during World War II.

A MAJOR STEP in the new era was the founding of the New Jersey Educational Review. From its very inception the Association had sought an official organ — communication with its membership is the greatest problem of any state or nationwide organization. We have seen how the Friends of Education attempted to make the New Jersey Life-Boat and Literary Standard an official organ. In its earliest years the State Teachers Association named the New York Teacher as its voice; Isaiah Peckham was New Jersey editor. In 1864 a report upon the subject of a "state educational journal" was made by Mr. E. C. Chapman.

"He spoke on the desirableness and necessity of such a journal as a medium of communication between teachers and for the general diffusion of educational intelligence. The subject was discussed in its educational and financial bearings by several members. It was moved that a committee of one from each county be appointed to canvass for subscribers to a monthly journal as indicated."

In 1867, State Superintendent Apgar recommended the establishment of an educational journal in the State, and a committee was appointed to consider the propriety of establishing one. A decade later Superintendent Apgar told the convention that the problem was solved by the establishment of the New Jersey Public School Journal, which was made the "official organ" and seems to have disappeared promptly. A year later, at any event, the teachers were being urged to subscribe to the New England Journal of Education.

With the turn of the century the Association published its annual proceedings and later, a list of members. This continued over a long period. In 1921 it again named an official organ, the School News of New Jersey, (later the New Jersey Journal of Education). This magazine was published in Newark for some 15 years under the editorship of Samuel Howe, a teacher in South Side High School. The financial arrangements between the Association and Mr. Howe are not clear; his June issue, however, became a special Association bulletin at a cost of $450. Most issues used a page for Association news, edited by a committee of three members. This arrangement lasted only five years; it was unsatisfactory, as most such arrangements prove to be. At the 1926 convention, the Association voted to publish its own magazine and a committee headed by Hubert R. Cornish of Paterson brought out the first issue in April, 1927. It was a quarterly, appearing in October, December, February and April.

PENSION PROBLEMS

While the new retirement system had been set up and put into operation, it demanded constant attention by its beneficiaries. In her book Pension Facts for Teachers, and in her other writing over a period of 30 years, Ida E. Housman has recorded the history of the Fund and of the work of the State Teachers Association to protect and improve it.

In the years between 1919 and 1926, the State at no time appropriated the amounts required by law for the Fund. In the first three years of that period the Trustees did not even certify the amounts needed. By 1922, however, Samuel H. McIlroy—a teacher trustee and the 1924 president of the Association—was voting against the certification on the ground that it was inadequate. When the Trustees finally did begin to certify the required amounts, the Legislature still failed to make the necessary appropriations. As they were to do again in the 1940's, the Trustees added to the ordinary certifications for a given year, the amounts unpaid from previous years. As a result the 1925 certification was $3,823,823 —a staggering sum at that time. To aid the State, the Association had a bill drafted to build the Fund's reserves more slowly. The bill was passed, and the certification substantially reduced, and the Legislature appropriated almost the amount certified. William J. Bickett of Trenton and Mr. Glennie of Newark were the key figures in this compromise.

A year later, however, the Legislature's Appropriations Committee again tried to reduce the appropriation by more than a million dollars. To enforce the terms of the compromise, the Association waged a vigorous campaign, with notable assistance from the press. On March 10, 1926, a hearing was held on the issue in the State House, Trenton, before the combined Judiciary and Appropriations Committees. President George J. Smith spoke for the teachers, supported by key political leaders and influential citizens. The full amount certified was put in the appropriations bill and paid. In the course of this struggle the State Association printed and distributed widely through the State a digest of editorial opinion and the complete minutes of the public hearing. As a result the appropriations from 1926 until 1932 were the amounts certified, and they were paid as due.

Criticism of the Fund persisted, however, since the whole concept of pensions and retirement was less familiar than now. In 1926 the Legislature created a special joint commission "to investigate the operation of the Fund." As Legislative Chairman for the Association, Mr. Glennie reported in 1927 that the special commission report established these points:

"1. The entire actuarial structure is sound, conservative and in harmony with the actual experience to date of the New Jersey teaching corps and similar teachers' pension funds.

"2. The benefits provided are sufficiently large to provide adequate protection after retirement and yet not so large as to make the cost prohibitive if sound methodical plans of financing obligations are used.

"3. The method of financing now in use is economical, equitable, and in the best interests of the State."

THIS THEN was the situation in 1929-30, when the depression came to New Jersey as to the rest of America. The Association had its headquarters office, with a small staff; it had established its magazine. It had won its first battles for the new retirement system; it had a clear set of legislative aims which were being presented to the Legislature each year through an active legislative committee; it was continuing its program of protecting the legal rights of individual teachers with financial assistance.

The effects of the depression were not immediately apparent. John H. Bosshart, later Commissioner of Education, was chairman of the Association's Committee on Educational Progress in the 1929-31 years. His reports in no way reflect the "hard times" that were beginning. They deal with such professional problems as publicity, teacher-training, the project method, creative activity, individualized instruction, grouping, promotion policies, the secondary curriculum, health, and education of the handicapped. Only obliquely, in a 1931 convention resolution, is there any reference to the need of maintaining educational services in the face of difficulties.

The first effects of the depression were local, of course. Communities were unable to collect taxes from the unemployed, they were unable to borrow from the banks the money they needed to pay teachers, they were failing to pay the retirement system the money supposedly withheld from teachers' salaries. They were turning to the State for help on their relief rolls.

PAYMENT BY SCRIP

Early in 1932, however, local pressure for reduced salaries resulted in a legislative move to relax the tenure act prohibition against salary cuts. This was met by a "march on Trenton" in which thousands of teachers poured into the State capital when the Legislature was considering this proposal. The proposal was defeated for the time being, only to reappear the following year.

By 1932 the Association was "fully recognizing the necessity for the most rigid economy during the present economic crisis." However, it resented bitterly a statement by Mayor Harry Bacharach of Atlantic City in greeting the convention. The mayor referred to the necessity of reducing educational costs, and stated that "the complex and highly specialized school curriculum probably could and should be simplified as one means of bringing about that reduction." The Association threatened not to take its future conventions to Atlantic City, and an apology of sorts was forthcoming.

By April 1933, the Review was carrying pictures of the scrip used to pay Atlantic City and Camden teachers, with a discussion of whether it helped or hurt the teachers who received it, and in October 1934 the Association president opened his message to members by saying "The past year has been a disastrous one in American education."

THE ASSOCIATION, however, met the challenge of hard times squarely. It had already taken the initial steps toward the state-wide survey of school financing to be known as the Mort Report. In 1932 it sought new and vigorous leadership by interrupting the regular succession of officers. As its head for the difficult years it chose Frank G. Pickell, the dynamic superintendent of the Montclair schools. He was the only president in its 100 years to be thrice-elected to the presidency, and his untiring efforts during difficult years in that office undoubtedly contributed to his early death. To finance a more vigorous program, it first asked for teacher contributions—collecting over $35,000 in two years—and then, when the clouds were darkest and thousands of teachers were failing to receive their salaries, it doubled its dues to $2.00 a year.

President Pickell moved quickly to meet the numerous attacks on education. He set up an Official News Bulletin to circulate information quickly throughout the State. Within a year this was incorporated into a complete overhaul of the Association's publications—the Review expanded to six issues a year, with a separate editorial office in the Griffith Building, Newark, and the writer of this material employed as editor. Within another year, an assistant editor was employed, and the editor assigned to field activities.

Efforts to defeat the "salary reduction" amendment to the tenure act were unsuccessful. The Association did defeat, with another "March on Trenton," a 1934 attempt to make a flat 25% cut in all local expenditures, including schools. Some 4,000 teachers and parents filled Trenton's War Memorial Building on that issue.

Without a doubt, however, the biggest contribution of the Association toward holding the line during the depression years was its advocacy of the Mort State School Aid plan. This saved education and the teachers from fighting a purely defensive battle; they had concrete, constructive proposals, and while the proposals themselves were never put into effect, the campaign for them undoubtedly saved the schools from much more severe cuts.

STATE AID

In 1921 a resolution noted that "it is the sense of the New Jersey State Teachers' Association that the State should increase the amount of money contributed by the State to the support of education." This resolution— or others like it—had been appearing regularly, almost from the very beginning of the Association. Conditions now, however, forced the Association to seek positive action in the state school aid field. The new pension law was being financed by the State out of railroad tax money, which had previously gone to local districts.

The Association had no clear-cut program, however. At a legislative hearing on a proposal to raise the state's 2.75 mill property tax to six mills, with distribution on the basis of teachers or children (rather than ratables,) the city and rural areas opposed each other bitterly. Under President Samuel H. McIlroy of Newark, the Association helped defeat a simple proposal to change the method of distribution to days attendance.

In 1923, however, President Preston H. Smith proposed a committee of nine "to make a complete study of the state school system." Apparently his idea had not been "sold" in advance; it provoked a storm of discussion. The development of state aid programs out of state-wide surveys was widespread, however, and when the depression began in 1929 the need of state financial help for school programs became especially acute.

In 1932 Governor A. Harry Moore announced that the New Jersey State Teachers' Association had "expressed its willingness to finance, out of its own funds, a fact-finding survey of New Jersey's educational system." He appointed a commission for that purpose, which organized under the chairmanship of Thomas N. McCarter, President of the Public Service Corporation, with Solomon C. Strong of West Orange, Association secretary, as its secretary. The commission consisted of thirteen "laymen" and eleven schoolmen and women.

Actually the Association had engaged Dr. Paul R. Mort to make the survey months before the Commission was appointed. Before it met, he had set up a Trenton office and gathered considerable material. The Commission agreed to accept Dr. Mort as its technician but insisted also on a survey of possible "economies"; eventually it approved the so-called Mort Survey of State Aid, which was released to public view in December 1933. It is noteworthy, however, that Chairman McCarter virtually disowned the report at the initial press conference upon it.

D ESPITE this set-back the Association plunged into an active campaign for the Mort proposals. In this it was strongly supported by the Federated Boards of Education, led by William J. Duffy of Hoboken and Charles Brown of Union City, and the Congress of Parents and Teachers, led by Mrs. William F. Little of Rahway. Presidents Pickell and Neulen toured the State explaining the recommendations of the Mort Commission.

As always, the controversy centered on the tax sources needed for the state support program. Hopes were high for a brief time in 1934 when Governor Harold G. Hoffman advocated a sales-income tax program. His sales tax was enacted, however, with no provision for using any of its revenue for schools. Under bitter opposition by the State Taxpayers Association, it was repealed after a few months. The fate of this sales tax was the background for the dominance of the Republican Party in New Jersey for the next fifteen years by its "Clean Government" wing, with a battle-cry of "No New Taxes." This blocked most moves in the direction of real state school aid, though the Association campaigned consistently for it and made it a peg for propaganda which undoubtedly helped the schools in many other ways.

In the 1935 Legislature there was strong support for the Mort proposals; to take advantage of it, the Association leaders agreed to the passage of the so-called Mort Plan bill, sponsored by Senator Joseph G. Wolber of Essex, to be effective "when and if" money for it was available. It became Chap. 224, P. L. 1935 and remained on the statutes for a decade, without ever being put into operation. From this experience the Association emerged with a strong prejudice against this type of conditional legislation.

Much of the bitter opposition to the Association's program in this period came from the New Jersey Taxpayers Association. The Taxpayers vigorously advocated limitation of local tax rates. This the education groups just as vigorously opposed. Epithets such as "School Lobby" and "Moneyed Interests" were freely exchanged in the press. The result, however, was a sort of stalemate —no state aid, no tax limitation.

DEPRESSION PENSIONS

The depression years were difficult ones, too, for the Pension Fund, and the State Association again had to justify its role as the watch-dog for its thousands of teacher-members. By 1932 the demands for relief funds were heavy on the Legislature, and there was little money in the State Treasury. A $20,000,000 bond issue was agreed on—to be voted in the November 1932 election. To meet immediate needs, the State "borrowed" at 4% the $4,161,566 due the Fund on July 1 of that year.

After the election, however, it was discovered that the wording of the Bond Act did not permit repayment of the "loan" from its proceeds. There was a sharp issue of good faith between the teachers and the legislators. Though friendly legislators offered bills to keep the promises that had been made, the State defaulted on its July 1933 payment to the Fund, making its total obligation over $8,500,000.

The State finally agreed to turn over to the Fund at par the State's bonds in the Delaware River Joint Commission. At the time these bonds were worth considerably less than their par value. After the depression was over, however, the Fund sold them at a substantial profit.

The struggle to obtain this solution illustrates the close relationship between the Association and the Trustees. As Association president Mr. Pickell wrote asking whether the failure to receive the State payments was dissipating the reserves of the teachers' own money. A few months later, apparently under Association pressure and on advice of their actuary, the Trustees threatened to suspend payments to teachers already retired. To secure the physical possession of the Delaware River bridge bonds, the Association offered to provide legal aid to the Trustees, who voted to accept such aid if the Attorney General refused to act for them. The $8,617,000 in bonds were transferred to the Trustees on December 18, 1933, less than a month before the suspension of pension payments was scheduled.

NEW DIFFICULTIES arose promptly. Contending that their taxes were unreasonably high, the railroads crossing New Jersey withheld payment. The State's obligations to the retirement system had been met out of these taxes. Beginning in 1934, the State made only partial payments to the Fund, despite the vigorous protests of the teachers. Dr. Leon N. Neulen of Camden, then Association president, wrote to the Trustees, "As an active member of the Fund, will you please assure me that in continuing to pay pensions to retired teachers, you are not dissipating reserves which you should hold for active members of the Fund: If you can give me no such assurance, will you please advise on what authority you are continuing to pay pensions with the State in default on its reserve contributions?"

Again the Trustees threatened to suspend pension payments. This time a "windfall" in the form of inheritance taxes on the large Dorrance estate came to the rescue. Legislation sponsored by Senator Charles E. Loizeaux (Union) authorized the use of $3,541,192.81 of the Dorrance money to meet the State's unpaid obligations. A third series of withholdings, failure to pay, and borrowings began immediately, however. This followed the previous pattern, and the State's accumulated obligations reached more than $8,000,000 by 1944, when the Association secured legislation providing for payment in full.

A FOURTH series of controversies between the State and the teachers began in 1947, when Governor Alfred E. Driscoll recommended a payment of only $1,500,000 a year to the so-called Deficiency account of the Fund, as against nearly $4,000,000 certified by the Trustees under the law to meet the State's obligations for the pre-1919 service of members. The State Association bitterly opposed the legislation to legalize the reduced payment, and for a five-year period we had the spectacle of the Trustees certifying each year the amount required under the 1926 law, while the Legislature appropriated only the $1,500,000 recommended by the Governor. Each year, too, the Trustees re-certified the amounts unpaid from previous years. Finally, in 1952, after a series of conferences in which the Association took the initiative, a compromise was reached. Annual payments of $2,000,000 for the Deficiency Account were agreed upon, and again the State started to meet in full its legal obligations to the Fund.

During this twenty-year period of almost continuous difficulty between the State and the teachers, it is worthy of note that the total assets of the Fund grew from $33,-000,000 to over $200,000,000. It should be noted, too, that near the end of this period, largely as a result of the 1947 constitution and the strong-Governor philosophy which underlay it, the authority of the Trustees was greatly weakened, despite vigorous protests by the State Association. By 1953 the Governor, through the State Treasurer, exercised a far more direct control over the administration of the Fund and the investment of its monies. One effect of this may be to give the teachers an even greater interest in the selection of future governors, an interest which can be exercised only through a united State Association.

THREE OTHER ACHIEVEMENTS of the depression
decade merit mention. One was the continued defense of
tenure. During the 1920's the tenure principle had been
increasingly accepted throughout the state; political parties included platform planks in its favor, and some 80%
of the teachers enjoyed tenure protection. The Association continued, through its Grievance and Redress Committee, to aid teachers where significant principles seemed to be involved. One of the most notable cases was
that of Mrs. Marion G. Rein of Riverside, which the
Association in 1932-33 fought through the Court of Errors and Appeals at heavy cost. This case involved a
supervising principal caught in the middle of a local
struggle and forced out on the basis of ridiculous charges
and inadequate evidence. The State Board said "if Mrs.
Rein could be dismissed, then the position of no supervising principal or principal is secure. For them the word
tenure would be a mockery. It does not surprise us . . .
that the State Teachers' Association came to her aid."

Certain rural areas, however, still refused to place
teachers under tenure; many resorted to the subterfuge
of requiring resignations at the end of a three-year period
and rehiring their teachers after a break of a few days
in the continuity of their employment. With the depression opposition to tenure increased throughout the State.
Boards were under great pressure to dismiss married
teachers and to hire local residents to replace those who
did not live in their communities.

In 1934 a ruling by the State Board of Education
threatened to upset the whole tenure structure. It held
that teachers under school-year (10-month) contracts,
rather than calendar-year contracts never attained the
three years of continuous employment required by the
act. The decision was made public on a Saturday; at the
Legislative session on the following Monday, the Association pushed through an amendment to cover the
"school year" contract and blanketing under tenure the
thousands of teachers affected.

Encouraged by its success, it tackled the problem of tenure evasions. After a two year campaign it secured, in 1940, an amendment which ended the phony-resignation method of breaking tenure.

CERTIFICATION

The Association took vigorous action in the area of teacher certification. In 1935 the State Board of Education adopted new certification rules which, in effect, wiped out the permanent certificates which teachers were given after three years of successful teaching. Under the new rules holders of such certificates could have been required to take added courses to meet the rising requirements for entrance into the profession. A special committee of the Association under Frank J. McMackin of Jersey City brought about a 1937 revision which did away with this requirement. The teachers contended that the validity of permanent certificates was essential to the tenure principle—as tenure is essential to a sound retirement plan. The furor over certification also resulted in changes in the membership of the State Board of Examiners to provide greatly increased teacher-representation.

In the 1940's the Association again took a vigorous interest in certification and teaching standards. Under the influence of the teacher shortage, emergency certificates were issued to teachers with far less than the qualifications desired. The Association, through the Long-Time Planning Committee, sought to maintain standards, to call the situation to the attention of the public, and to encourage, through a "Future Teacher" program, young people to enter the profession. As its first century ended, the Association played a leading role in obtaining a $15,000,000 bond issue for expansion of the State Teachers Colleges.

A third major achievement was legislation requiring boards to protect teachers from lawsuits growing out of their professional activities. This resulted from a number of damage claims by parents of pupils injured in normal physical education activities. Boards were first required to provide the teachers with legal counsel; later the law was changed to require that they save the teacher harmless from such suits. As a result of this legislation boards now carry insurance covering such accidents.

To THIS PERIOD too, belongs the record of the Association's campaign for minimum salaries. Agitation for such a law began at the beginning of the century. It was laid aside, however, and only revived in the inflationary period after World War I. The first minimum salary bill was passed in 1919, providing for a minimum of $70 a month. This was only $630 a year, since the legal requirement was for a nine-month term.

During the 1920's this seemed so low that there was little disposition to change the law. In 1930 only 14 teachers in the State were receiving the minimum. With the depression, however, more districts reverted to it, and the number of teachers on the minimum increased rapidly.

In 1936, with the law permitting salary cuts under tenure barely off the books, the Association started to back legislation for a $1,000 minimum. By persistent efforts that was achieved, and pushed up to $1200 a year early in World War II. Under the post-war inflation, the minimum again rose, first to $1800, and then, by a series of annual increases, to the present figure of $2500.

Interest in some form of *schedule*—a series of minimums based on experience—appeared as early as 1919. It developed little support, however, until the late 1940's. Not until 1950 did it become an established objective of the Association.

DEMOCRATIZATION

Association control was—and remained for another decade—in the hands of a relatively small group of leaders, who were widely known and recognized as the pillars of the Association. They led the Association ably, and with continuing concern for its good and for the welfare of all the teachers, but their strength lay in their recognition by their fellow-leaders, rather than in a process of democratic selection.

Each was presumed, within the group, to speak for the teachers of a given area. Eminent among them, in the 1920's were Superintendents Charles B. Boyer of Atlantic City, William J. Bickett of Trenton, and somewhat later, Mr. Strong of West Orange and Burton Patrick of Orange. Also important were a few principals, notably William A. Wetzel of Trenton, Alexander J. Glennie and Raymond B. Gurley of Newark.

On matters of major importance, however, the leaders would call in a much larger group. The annual selection of a slate of candidates for officers of the Association was an occasion for the larger meetings. These were not placid sessions; sometimes they involved bitter arguments. Rarely, however, did those who attended fail to support the agreed-on policy.

I N THE 1930's, this method of operation began to break down. It was attacked from two sides. The elementary women teachers, through the Classroom Teachers Association, sought a greater voice in the control and policy-making of the Association, without serious disagreement over the Association policies themselves. Such leaders as Mattie Doremus of Paterson, Mrs. Mary D. Barnes of Elizabeth, and Lelia O. Brown of Newark served on the Executive Committee of the Association and vigorously supported moves for disseminating information to teachers, more active public relations and field work, and more democratic operation of the Association.

At the same time a group of urban teachers, mostly from the high schools, sharply criticized the policies of the Association as not progressive enough. Newark, where the local association for several years employed its own Executive Secretary, was the center of the latter movement. This group pressed for major changes in Association leadership, and offered, without success, candidates for the presidency in 1935, 1937, 1938 and 1939.

It was evident that there was strong sentiment throughout the State for some reorganization of the Association, and considerable feeling that the time was ripe for a full-time Executive Secretary. As early as 1934 resolutions were introduced asking for an executive secretary and a new method of nominating the Association officers. In an effort to meet these requests, the Executive Committee employed an assistant editor for the magazine, and successively gave the editor additional duties as Field Secretary, publicity director, and Coordinating Assistant to the President.

After a few unsuccessful attempts to amend the constitution, a committee headed by William L. Fidler of Audubon spent two years on a complete revision. The result was adopted in 1938. It changed the name of the Association to the New Jersey Education Association, enlarged the Executive Committee to represent all counties, and set up a policy-making Delegate Assembly, with the county representatives on both groups elected back in the counties. The Convention itself added mail voting to the changes.

Dr. Fidler was elected President to put the changes into effect. The Delegate Assembly—originally intended to meet only at the Convention—held advisory sessions which soon became official. County organizations were granted the right to participate in the elections of county representatives, and the mail ballot—first proposed for the benefit of those unable to attend the convention— became the preferred method of voting. In 1952 the method of mail voting was simplified.

THE TENSIONS within the Association were not, however, ended by the new constitution. They flared again in a sharply contested presidential election in 1941, and over Executive Committee procedures when Mrs. Applegate was retired in 1940 after 17 years of service. The Committee sought to draw the Association closer together by a complete staff reorganization. Dr. Charles

DR. CHARLES J. STRAHAN

J. Strahan, Deputy Commissioner of Education after a long career in New Jersey schools, was generally admired and respected by New Jersey teachers. He was induced to succeed Mrs. Applegate as Executive Clerk, with the implied promise that he would be made Executive Secretary. Dr. Strahan himself was completely above and outside Association controversies.

Resenting the fact that it had not been consulted about the changes, however, the Delegate Assembly "censured" the President and 17 members of the Executive Committee for "hasty and ill-considered action in forcing a fundamental change in the policy of the Association, refusing to permit opportunity for discussion and deliberation on the part of the Delegate Assembly and the membership of the Association." It made clear, however, that it approved the Executive Secretaryship and was in no way reflecting upon Dr. Strahan personally.

That resolution was in fact a declaration of independence by the Delegate Assembly. It established clearly, early in the life of the Delegate Assembly, its determination to be consulted on Association policy; that right has never since been questioned. On the other hand, the wisdom of the Executive Committee's choice was borne out by the fact that a very genuine "era of good feeling" has persisted since that time in the conduct of Association affairs. On most matters the Executive Committee and the Delegate Assembly have seen eye to eye. and most decisions on significant questions by both bodies have been nearly unanimous. Much of this was undoubtedly due to Dr. Strahan's own personality, his ability to bring opposing groups together in the spirit of compromise, and his unquestioned personal integrity.

THE LAST DECADE

In addition to the good feeling that was developing within the Association under Mr. Strahan as Executive Secretary, two other events of this period are significant. In an effort to improve public relations and general understanding of the schools, the Association approved a program offered by its Long-Time Planning Committee under Dr. Edgar L. Finck of Toms River. Known as "Democratic Discussions," it envisioned, on a state-wide basis, a series of teacher-sponsored, teacher-led discussions by citizens of topics of current interest. usually with a more or less direct bearing on education.

To finance this program the members of the Association paid assessments of some $10,000. To operate it the Association employed Dr. Frederick L. Hipp. then in his early 30's. The outbreak of war almost before the program was launched handicapped the project by transportation difficulties and the multitude of war activities in which people were involved. Dr. Hipp himself was gradually withdrawn from its leadership, first to edit the Review and then to carry on a broader public relations program.

DR. FREDERICK L. HIPP

As president Dr. Fidler recognized the need of a new approach to state school aid. Hope was dimming that the Mort Plan could be made effective. A government-study group centered at Princeton was making broad studies of State finance. To cooperate with it, Dr. Fidler appointed a special committee headed by Dr. John H. Bosshart. Out of this grew, over a few years, a new state school aid program. Offered to the Legislature in 1944, it spurred the appointment of a Legislative Commission headed by Senator Herbert J. Pascoe of Union, and with Dr. Bosshart—by then Commissioner of Education—as Secretary. This commission produced a state aid plan—the Pascoe Act—which was adopted in 1946, after a vigorous state-wide campaign financed by the

Association and operating through an Educational Planning Commission with Dr. Hipp as secretary.

The times conspired, however, to make the Pascoe Act inadequate almost before it took effect. When the war ended in 1945, a sharp inflation was piled on top of the slow rise in costs that had gone on during the war. Many teachers were in the armed services, and the post-war increase in births accentuated the teacher-shortage. These factors—especially the inflation—produced a period of unparalleled tension among teachers. Desperate at the failure of 1939 salaries to meet 1945-46 living costs, teachers turned anywhere they could for help. In some places there was talk of strikes, and most of the teachers of Paterson—in protest at woefully inadequate salaries —reported "sick" on the same day in February, 1946.

The Association met this challenge bravely. Dr. Hipp was assigned virtually full-time to the task of helping local groups meet their problems, and of preaching the gospel to others that unified action through strong State and local organizations was better than disunity. In the Paterson situation, especially, he won major concessions for the teachers, and developed an "NJEA approach" to field work and public relations that won national acceptance. In local situations where teachers and boards had reached a stalemate, the NJEA representative would serve as a fusing agent, helping the local group to frame carefully its objectives and the reasons for them, then bringing teachers, board-members, and often-times citizen representatives around a conference table to seek agreements.

By 1946, when Mr. Strahan was ready to retire as Executive Secretary, Dr. Hipp was a natural choice as his successor. He accepted his new responsibility with a virtually new staff, the Review editor just back from four years in the army, and two newly employed field representatives.

The achievements since 1946 hardly need be detailed here. They include increased State school aid (out of cigarette tax money in 1947) and continuous campaigns for the further increases made necessary by rising school costs; liberalization of teacher retirement in the direction of the 35-year, half-pay goal set nearly half a century before; expansion of the field service-public relations program until the Association now serves directly hundreds of local and county associations each year; the addition of a research director to the NJEA staff; and in 1951 the purchase by the Association of its own attractive headquarters building at 180 W. State Street, Trenton—directly opposite the State House.

It should be obvious then that the New Jersey Education Association will face its second century immeasurably stronger and better able to serve its membership than it was at any time during the first hundred years; and with no less determination to do the things which need doing, than it had when that small group met in Bayard Street School, New Brunswick in 1853.

FORMER PRESIDENTS OF THE
NEW JERSEY EDUCATION ASSOCIATION

(from the doctorate thesis (Rutgers) of
Dr. James C. Montgomery)

Year	President	Residence	Place of Meeting
1853	Robert Latimer Cooke	Bloomfield	New Brunswick
1854	Robert Latimer Cooke	Bloomfield	Trenton
1855	Robert Latimer Cooke	Bloomfield	Trenton, Newark
1856	J. Sandford Smith	Sussex	Bridgeton
1857	Isaiah Peckham	Newark	Trenton
1858	William F. Phelps	Trenton	Jersey City
1859	B. Harrison	Morris County	No Record
1860	F. W. Ricord	Newark	No Record
1861	William F. Phelps	Trenton	Newark
1862	S. C. Hosford	Paterson	Bridgeton
1863	S. A. Farrand	Sussex	New Brunswick
1864	C. M. Harrison	Middlesex	Rahway
1865	H. B. Pierce	Mercer	Hackettstown
1866	Robert H. DeHart	Warren	No Meeting
1867	Robert H. Dehart	Warren	Plainfield
1868	Joseph E. Haynes	Essex	Moorestown
1869	Samuel Lockwood	Monmouth	Moorestown
1870	W. A. Breckenridge	—	Camden
1871	George B. Sears	Essex	Newark
1872	—	—	No Meeting
1873	W. N. Barringer	Newark	Vineland
1874	W. N. Barringer	Newark	Trenton
1875	F. R. Brace	Camden County	Trenton
1876	M. H. Martin	Trenton	Trenton
1877	Edmond Hovey	Newark	New Brunswick
1878	J. F. Street	Beverly	Asbury Park
1879	George H. Barton	Jersey City	Long Branch
1880	G. O. F. Taylor	Essex	Long Branch
1881	J. M. Green	Long Branch	Long Branch
1882	William L. Dickinson	Jersey City	Newark
1883	Randall Spaulding*	Montclair	Newark
1884	B. Homes	Elizabeth	Newark
1885	Charles Jacobus	New Brunswick	Newark
1886	Clarence E. Meleney	Paterson	Trenton
1887	Austin C. Apgar	Trenton	Trenton
1888	William M. Griffin	Newark	Trenton
1889	A. B. Guilford	Jersey City	Trenton

Page 106

NJEA Presidents

Year	President	Residence	Place of Meeting
1890	Silas R. Morse	Atlantic City	Trenton
1891	E. H. Cooke	New Brunswick	Asbury Park
1892	Addison B. Poland	Newark	Asbury Park
1893	John Enright	Freehold	No Meeting
1894	John Enright	Freehold	No Meeting
1895	H. Brewster Willis	New Brunswick	No Meeting
1896	S. Ervin Manness	Newark	Trenton
1897	J. Howard Hulsart	Dover	Trenton
1898	Henry W. Maxson	Plainfield	Trenton
1899	F. Thorn	Paterson	Jersey City
1900	Edwin Shepard	Newark	Newark
1901	Langdon Thompson	Jersey City	Trenton
1902	Charles J. Baxter	Plainfield	Trenton
1903	William H. Eldridge	Williamstown	Trenton
1904	W. Collom Cook	Mount Holly	Trenton
1905	William M. Swingle	Orange	Atlantic City
1906	Henry Snyder	Jersey City	Atlantic City
1907	Charles B. Boyer	Atlantic City	Atlantic City
1908	James E. Bryan	Camden	Atlantic City
1909	Ebenezer Mackey	Trenton	Atlantic City
1910	J. J. Savitz	Westfield	Atlantic City
1911	Powell G. Fithian	Camden	Atlantic City
1912	George Morris	Bloomfield	Atlantic City
1913	H. J. Neal	Bridgeton	Atlantic City
1914	Elizabeth A. Allen	Hoboken	Atlantic City
1915	William A. Wetzel	Trenton	Atlantic City
1916	Frank H. Lloyd	Perth Amboy	Atlantic City
1917	Albert Moncrief	Jersey City	Atlantic City
1918	Henry M. Cressman	Egg Harbor City	Atlantic City
1919	Alexander J. Glennie	Newark	Atlantic City
1920	Ide G. Sargeant	Paterson	Atlantic City
1921	J. J. Unger	Vineland	Atlantic City
1922	Preston H. Smith	Bayonne	Trenton
1923	Preston H. Smith	Bayonne	Newark
1924	Samuel H. McIlroy	Newark	Atlantic City
1925	William J. Bickett	Trenton	Atlantic City
1926	George J. Smith	Clifton	Atlantic City
1927	George R. Gerard	Belleville	Atlantic City
1928	Henry P. Miller	Atlantic City	Atlantic City
1929	Raymond B. Gurley	Newark	Atlantic City
1930	George C. Baker	Moorestown	Atlantic City
1931	Adele Cox	Jersey City	Atlantic City

Year	President	Residence	Place of Meeting
1932	Chester F. Ogden	Clifton	Atlantic City
1933	Frank G. Pickell	Montclair	Atlantic City
1934	Frank G. Pickell	Montclair	Atlantic City
1935	Frank G. Pickell	Montclair	Atlantic City
1936	Leon N. Neulen	Camden	Atlantic City
1937	Leon N. Neulen	Camden	Atlantic City
1938	Sarah O. Whitlock	New Brunswick	Atlantic City
1939	William L. Fidler	Audubon	Atlantic City
1940	William L. Fidler	Audubon	Atlantic City
1941	Lelia O. Brown	Newark	Atlantic City
1942	Lelia O. Brown	Newark	Trenton
1943	Charles A. Philhower	Westfield	New York City
1944	Charles A. Philhower	Westfield	New York City
1945	Charles A. Philhower	Westfield	Atlantic City
1946	Bertha Lawrence	Trenton	Atlantic City
1947	Bertha Lawrence	Trenton	Atlantic City
1948	Charles L. Steel, Jr.	Teaneck	Atlantic City
1949	Charles L. Steel, Jr.	Teaneck	Atlantic City
1950	Mrs. Florence H. Price	Newark	Atlantic City
1951	Mrs. Florence H. Price	Newark	Atlantic City
1952	William R. Stover	Pennsauken	Atlantic City
1953	William R. Stover	Pennsauken	

*Elizabeth A. Allen was 2nd Vice President

NJEA AWARD FOR

DISTINGUISHED SERVICE TO EDUCATION

The purpose of the Award is to call public attention to those citizens of the State who, from time to time, shall greatly serve the schools, and through them the children of the State. It is also the purpose of this Award to demonstrate that the Association, and its members as teachers, believe that service to education is one of the highest forms of service any citizen or citizens can give.

1934—ALEXANDER JOHN GLENNIE
1935—JOSEPH C. WOLBER
1936—MRS. WILLIAM F. LITTLE
1937—ARTHUR N. PIERSON
1938—DR. CLARENCE E. PARTCH
1939—CHARLES A. BROWN
1940—MRS. STELLA S. APPLEGATE
1941—W. BURTON PATRICK
1942—EDWARD CAREY MARKHAM
1943—ENSIGN MARGARET YOUNG ELMER, USNR
      LIEUT. ALVIN A. FRY, U. S. Army
Emblematical Award on behalf of men and women of New
      Jersey in the Military Services

1944—no award
1945—no award
1946—MATTIE S. DOREMUS
1947—NEW JERSEY PRESS ASSOCIATION
1948—GRACE M. FREEMAN
      E. MORGAN BARRADALE
1949—HERBERT J. PASCOE
1950—NEW JERSEY CONGRESS OF PARENTS AND TEACHERS
1951—HAROLD RAY
1952—BERTHA LAWRENCE

This history of the New Jersey Education originally appeared in the New Jersey Educational Review in December 1952, January, February and March 1953, in connection with the Centennial Observance of the Association. It was written by Laurence B. Johnson, Editor of the Review, and an employee of the Association since 1934.

The writer gladly acknowledges his debt to James D. Montgomery of Rutherford, who wrote his Rutgers doctorate thesis on the history of the Association. Other significant sources are the report of the early Superintendents of Schools, the Association's own minutes, and such historians of New Jersey education as Murray, Raum, Dr. Ellis A Apgar, Dr. Ira Chapman, and Dr. Nelson K. Burr.